Ma Ke ʻAno Kūloko

Healthy Cooking — Island Style

Sponsored by Project LEAN Hawaiʻi

Funding and in-kind donations generously contributed by:

The Queen's Medical Center Dietitians
Written and developed by:

Lisa Bravo, R.D.
Cherilyn Hawthorn, R.D.
Betsy Solazzo, R.D.
Judy Thompson, M.P.H., R.D.
Diana Valle, R.D.

Hawaii Medical Service Association
Design, Production and Printing:

Coordinator
Alicia Chan

Art Direction
Candace Fenander

Production Artists
Jean Au
Lawrence Pascua

Illustrations
Garry Ono

Hawaiian translations by:
Section headings: Pūnana Leo o Honolulu

Copy Editor
Marlene Sueyoshi

Project LEAN Hawai'i

*Dedicated to
the people of Hawai'i*

Table of Contents

Preface

Eating too much fat has been linked to many chronic health problems such as heart disease, diabetes, obesity and certain types of cancer. Project LEAN (Low-fat Eating for America Now) America is a national public awareness campaign which promotes low-fat eating. As part of its efforts to help the people of Hawaii eat less fat, Project LEAN Hawaii has created Ma Ke 'Ano Kuloko, Healthy Cooking—Island Style.

The latest U.S. Food and Drug Administration guidelines specify that to be called "lean," an entree containing meat or meat substitute, poultry or fish should have no more than 9 grams of fat per serving. Side dishes such as vegetables and desserts should have no more than 3 grams of fat per serving. A "reduced fat" dish should have 25 percent less fat than the original dish.

Ma Ke 'Ano Kuloko contains recipes which are naturally low in fat, along with recipes which have been modified to lower their fat content to meet the FDA's definition of "lean." In addition, each section begins with several reduced-fat recipes. All recipes have been taste tested and evaluated. Nutritional analyses and diabetic exchanges are provided for each recipe, using Nutritionist III and Food Processor II programs. Many dishes in the book may fit nicely into a low-sodium diet. You'll also find nutrition information and tips for low-fat cooking in the appendix.

Project LEAN Hawaii hopes you'll enjoy eating healthy, island-style, with Ma Ke 'Ano Kuloko.

Eating Lean

Health authorities recommend that we eat 30 percent or less of our total daily calories from fat. How much fat is this? The number of calories a person needs depends on a number of factors such as age, activity level and body size. Most adults need between 1,500 and 2,500 calories each day. The following chart lists the fat limits for this calorie range:

Total Calories Consumed each Day	Daily Fat Intake
1,500	50 grams
2,000	65 grams
2,500	80 grams

Daily fat intake includes fat and oil that is found naturally in food, such as chicken skin or oil in peanut butter, as well as the amount of fat that is added to food in the cooking process, such as oil for frying.

Most people can eat "lean" dishes on a daily basis and stay within their recommended fat limit. Reduced-fat dishes may need to be used less often.

Acknowledgements

The Queen's Medical Center dietitians would like to express a warm mahalo to all who contributed their time, recipes and helpful tips.

Misako Allen
Marie Baysa
Christine Beck
R.E. Black Memorial Trust
Joyce Blakeman
Carol Bledsoe
Cathy Borski
Trish Britten
Marianne Bueno
Gary Craft
Renee Mae Cuestas
Lisa Ann Dalida
Linda Dawson
Claire Doi
Josephine Endrina
Candace Fenander
Margie Gorospe
Barbara Gray
Suki Hamayashi
Virginia Hee
Kimberly Hew
Eileen Hirata
Herbert Hoe
Claire Hughes

Chizuko Ishii
Carol Ishizaki
Mae Isonaga
Sayuri Itahashi
Naomi Kanehiro
Ellen Katoda
Ronald Kawano
Stanley Kimura
Donna King-Davenport
Virginia Koo
Amy Kuraoka-Goo
Nancy Lance
Nancy Levenson
Allison Lum
Georgette Magnuson
Kelly Malone
Lisa Morita
Betty Nakagawa
Mary Nakasuji-Yoshino
Vivian Nishimoto
Shari Okimoto
Iris Oda
Judith Payne
Tyrone Shawn Peeples
J. Peters

David Reardon
Raenell Reyla
Michael Rufino
Caryn Shima
Carol Stevens
Lindy Styer
Marlene Sueyoshi
Pauline Sumida
Ann Sutherland
Milagros Tangaro
David Y. Tasaka
Stacy Taylor
Nancy Thomas
Betty Jo Thompson
Brenda Vincent
Katrina Vutnoski
Eva Young
Jerri Warne
John J. Wheeler
Rainbow Wong
Karen Wun
Julia Zee

Special thanks to Lisa Miller.
M.P.H., R.D., for nutritional analyses.

Nā mea hōʻonoʻono

Appetizers

Stuffed Mushrooms

Original

2 pounds (about 30) fresh mushrooms
3 stalks celery, finely chopped
8 sticks or 4 ounces imitation crab, finely chopped
1 cup mayonnaise
$1/2$ teaspoon salt
$1/4$ teaspoon pepper
1 cup panko (flour meal for breading)

Reduced

2 pounds (about 30) fresh mushrooms
3 stalks celery, finely chopped
8 sticks or 4 ounces imitation crab, finely chopped
1 cup reduced-calorie mayonnaise
$1/2$ teaspoon salt
$1/4$ teaspoon pepper
1 cup panko (flour meal for breading)

Remove stems from mushrooms. Finely chop half of the stems and combine with celery, crab, mayonnaise, salt, pepper and $1/2$ cup panko. Stuff mushrooms with mixture, building a slight mound. Place on cookie sheet and sprinkle with remainder of panko. Broil for 5 minutes or until lightly browned.

Nutritional Information *(per 2 mushroom serving)* Diabetic Exchanges

Original		Reduced		Original		Reduced	
Calories	150	Calories	95	Vegetable	1.5	Vegetable	2
Fat	12 g	Fat	6 g	Fat	2.5	Fat	1
Cholesterol	6 mg	Cholesterol	6 mg				
Sodium	234 mg	Sodium	271 mg				

Spinach Rolls

Original

   2 (10-ounce) boxes frozen chopped spinach
$^1/_2$ cup chopped green onion
   1 cup mayonnaise
   1 cup sour cream
   1 package ranch dressing mix
$^1/_2$ cup bacon bits
10 large flour tortillas

Reduced

   2 (10-ounce) boxes frozen chopped spinach
$^1/_2$ cup chopped green onion
   1 cup reduced-calorie mayonnaise
   1 cup non-fat sour cream
   1 package ranch dressing mix
$^1/_2$ cup bacon bits
10 large flour tortillas

Cook spinach until slightly tender, drain and squeeze to remove excess water. Combine remaining ingredients and spread evenly on tortilla. Roll into cylindrical shape. Cut each roll into 8 pieces.

Nutritional Information *(per 2 piece serving)*

Original		Reduced	
Calories	100	Calories	75
Fat	7 g	Fat	3 g
Cholesterol	6 mg	Cholesterol	2 mg
Sodium	162 mg	Sodium	191 mg

Diabetic Exchanges

Original		Reduced	
Vegetable	2.0	Vegetable	2.0
Fat	1.5	Fat	0.5

California Rolls

Original

 6 cups (use rice cooker measure) uncooked rice
 6 sticks or 3 ounces imitation crab
 1 Japanese cucumber
 1/2 small avocado
 3/4 cup mayonnaise
 1 1/2 teaspoons salt
 6 sheets nori
 3 teaspoons wasabi

Reduced

 6 cups (use rice cooker measure) uncooked rice
 6 sticks or 3 ounces imitation crab
 1 Japanese cucumber
 1/2 small avocado
 3/4 cup reduced-calorie mayonnaise
 1 1/2 teaspoons salt
 6 sheets nori
 3 teaspoons wasabi

Cook rice. Meanwhile, prepare sushi ingredients. Split imitation crab sticks in half lengthwise. Cut cucumber in half crosswise, then cut each half lengthwise into 8 sticks. Cut avocado lengthwise into 12 strips. Mix mayonnaise with salt. To roll sushi, place nori smooth side facing down on bamboo mat, with edge nearest you even with edge of mat. Cover 3/4 of nori sheet with 1 1/2 cups rice (about 1/2-inch thickness), leaving the end farthest away from you free of rice. Spread 2 tablespoons mayonnaise mixture over rice, then 1/2 teaspoon wasabi in a 1/2-inch line in the middle. Place 2 pieces imitation crab on wasabi, then arrange 2 slices each of cucumber and avocado on either side of crab. Roll sushi away from you, keeping filling in place with your fingers. Cut into 8 pieces.

Nutritional Information *(per 2 piece serving)* — Diabetic Exchanges

Original		Reduced		Original		Reduced	
Calories	150	Calories	125	Vegetable	1	Vegetable	1
Fat	6 g	Fat	3 g	Bread	1	Bread	1
Cholesterol	3 mg	Cholesterol	3 mg	Fat	1	Fat	0.5
Sodium	218 mg	Sodium	236 mg				

Chex Party Mix

Original

2 cups butter

1/8 tsp salt

1 tablespoon Worcestershire sauce

3/4 cup sugar

1 teaspoon garlic powder

1 (16-ounce) box wheat Chex

1 (12-ounce) box corn Chex

1 (14 1/2-ounce) box Honeycomb cereal

1 (10-ounce) package pretzels

1 (24-ounce) can peanuts

Reduced

1 3/4 cups margarine

1/8 teaspoon salt

1 tablespoon Worcestershire sauce

3/4 cup sugar

1 teaspoon garlic powder

1 (16-ounce) box wheat Chex

1 (12-ounce) box corn Chex

1 (14 1/2-ounce) box Honeycomb cereal

1 (10-ounce) package non-fat pretzels

1 (12-ounce) canned unsalted peanuts

Preheat oven to 250 degrees. Melt margarine and add salt, Worcestershire sauce, sugar and garlic powder. Bring to a boil over medium heat. Combine cereals, pretzels and nuts; pour margarine mixture over all and mix gently. Bake for 1 hour, stirring every 15 minutes

Nutritional Information (per 1 cup serving)

Original		Reduced	
Calories	295	Calories	245
Fat	16 g	Fat	11 g
Cholesterol	22 mg	Cholesterol	0 mg
Sodium	459 mg	Sodium	385 mg

Diabetic Exchanges

Original		Reduced	
Bread	2	Bread	2
Fat	3	Fat	2

Blackened Ahi

  Non-stick cooking spray
4 (4-ounce) ahi steaks
$^1/_4$ cup Cajun spice
2 cups shredded cabbage

Sauce:
$^1/_4$ cup low-sodium shoyu
$^1/_4$ cup dry mustard
$^1/_4$ cup prepared mustard
$^1/_4$ cup beer

Heat a heavy skillet for 7 minutes over high heat. Lightly coat each side of ahi steaks with non-stick cooking spray and coat completely with Cajun spice. Sear for one minute on each side. Thinly slice fish and place on bed of cabbage. Mix sauce ingredients well; serve on the side for dipping or pour directly over fish.

Nutritional Information		Diabetic Exchanges	
(per serving)			
Calories	115	Lean meat	2
Fat	3 g		
Cholesterol	27 mg		
Sodium	500 mg		

Fish Poke

1 pound fresh fish of your choice, cut into
   $^3/_4$-inch cubes

$^1/_2$ cup chopped green onion

2 Hawaiian chili peppers, seeded and minced

1 pound limu (blanched or raw), chopped bite-size

1 teaspoon inamona (prepared kukui nut sold at
   many large grocery stores, Ala Moana Farmers'
   Market and in Chinatown on Oahu)

Mix all ingredients together and chill.

Nutritional Information		Diabetic Exchanges	
(per serving)			
Calories	110	Vegetable	1
Fat	3 g	Lean meat	2
Cholesterol	27 mg		
Sodium	42 mg		

Hawaiian-Style Aku Poke

2 aku fillets (about 4 ounces each), skin and
   bones removed

1/2 small Maui onion, thinly sliced

2 tablespoons thinly sliced green onion

2 teaspoons minced ginger

1–2 small Hawaiian chili peppers, seeded and chopped

1/4 cup low-sodium shoyu

2 teaspoons sesame oil

Salt to taste

1 teaspoon sesame seeds

Cut aku into 3/4-inch cubes. In a large bowl, combine aku, Maui onion, green onion, ginger, chili pepper, shoyu, sesame oil and salt; mix lightly. Chill for several hours. Toast sesame seeds by heating in a heavy frying pan, stirring constantly until lightly browned. Sprinkle over poke and serve.

Nutritional Information

(per serving)

Calories	60
Fat	2 g
Cholesterol	15 mg
Sodium	402 mg

Diabetic Exchanges

Vegetable	0.5
Lean meat	1.0
Fat	0.5

Tofu Poke

1 large block firm tofu, drained and
  cut into 1-inch cubes

2 teaspoons toasted sesame seeds

1/4 cup coarsely chopped limu

2 tablespoons chopped green onion

1 teaspoon grated ginger

1/2 large red chili pepper, seeded and chopped

1/4 cup low-sodium shoyu

1 tablespoon sesame oil

Place tofu cubes in a colander to drain well, then place in a serving bowl. Sprinkle sesame seeds, limu, green onion, ginger and chili pepper over tofu cubes and toss lightly. Mix shoyu and sesame oil, then pour over the rest of the ingredients. Toss lightly and chill for 30 minutes.

Nutritional Information		Diabetic Exchanges	
(per serving)			
Calories	90	Vegetable	0.5
Fat	6 g	Medium-fat meat	1.0
Cholesterol	0 mg		
Sodium	361 mg		

Shrimp Summer Rolls

1 package rice sticks

1 package rice paper

1 head red leaf lettuce, shredded

1 bunch fresh basil

1 bunch fresh mint

1 carrot, grated

1 cucumber, grated

1 bunch green onion (green part only) in 2-inch lengths

1 pound cooked shrimp, halved lengthwise

Dipping sauce:

 2 tablespoons fish sauce

 2 tablespoons sugar

 2 tablespoons lemon juice

 2 cloves garlic, minced

 $1/2$ teaspoon garlic chili paste

 $2/3$ cup water

Boil rice sticks for about 4 minutes and drain well. Combine dipping sauce ingredients and set aside. Fill a large bowl with tap water. Dip rice paper quickly in water to soften, then lay it on a work surface. Place about 2 tablespoons noodles, some vegetables, herbs and two pieces shrimp on lower third of wrapper, leaving a 1-inch space along bottom and sides. Fold bottom up around filling, then fold left and right sides toward center. Continue to roll until a cylinder is formed. Place seam-side down on platter. Serve with dipping sauce. Makes 10 rolls.

Note: Rice paper may become soft and tear if too wet. Also, too much filling makes it difficult to roll.

Nutritional Information		Diabetic Exchanges	
(per 1 roll serving)			
Calories	145	Vegetable	1
Fat	0 g	Bread	1
Cholesterol	92 mg	Lean meat	1
Sodium	204 mg		

Hot and Spicy Chicken Siu Mai

1½ pounds coarsely ground chicken

¾ cup finely chopped Chinese cabbage

⅓ cup dried sliced shiitake mushroom

4 slices ginger, minced (approximately 1½ tablespoons)

1 tablespoon rice wine or sherry

2 tablespoons oyster sauce

2 tablespoons chili sauce with garlic

2 teaspoons sesame oil

¼ cup chopped green onion

½–1 teaspoon cayenne pepper

1 tablespoon cornstarch

¼ cup grated carrots

2 (12-ounce) packages won ton wrappers

Dipping Sauce:

½ cup low-sodium shoyu

2 tablespoons apple cider vinegar

Soak shiitake mushrooms in warm water for 10 minutes. Drain, squeeze out excess water and mince. Combine ground chicken and remaining ingredients except won ton wrappers. Dip won ton wrappers in water, shake off excess. Place 1 tablespoon of filling in center. Gather edges to form pleats, leaving top open. Flatten bottom while placing in 9-inch cake pans lightly coated with non-stick cooking spray. Leave a ½-inch space between each siu mai. Steam on medium-high heat for 8 minutes. Serve with dipping sauce.

Nutritional Information		*Diabetic Exchanges*	
(per 1 piece serving)			
Calories	35	Lean meat	0.5
Fat	2 g		
Cholesterol	11 mg		
Sodium	83 mg		

Salsa

  2 (16-ounce) cans tomatoes, drained

  6 stalks green onion, chopped

1–3 teaspoons chopped garlic

  1 (4-ounce) can diced green chiles, mild or hot

  3 tablespoons chopped Chinese parsley

Combine all ingredients in a food processor or blender. Process on "chop" for 15 to 30 seconds, depending on desired consistency. Salsa can be frozen for later use.

Nutritional Information

(per ¼ cup serving)

Calories	25
Fat	0 g
Cholesterol	0 mg
Sodium	50 mg

Diabetic Exchanges

Vegetable	1

Kim Chee Dip

$^1/_2$ cup chopped kim chee
1 tablespoon kim chee liquid
1 (8-ounce) package low-fat cream cheese

Blend ingredients in a food processor for 1 minute. Chill and serve with vegetable sticks or crackers.

Nutritional Information		Diabetic Exchanges	
(per 1 tablespoon serving)			
Calories	30	Fat	0.5
Fat	3 g		
Cholesterol	5 mg		
Sodium	109 mg		

Salmon and Water Chestnut Dip

Serves 6

1 (16-ounce) can salmon, drained, bones removed and flaked

1 cup non-fat sour cream

1 (8-ounce) can water chestnuts, drained and finely chopped

2 tablespoons finely chopped green onion

1 tablespoon shoyu

Fresh parsley, chopped (optional)

Mix all ingredients except parsley. Cover and refrigerate at least 2 hours. Garnish with chopped parsley. Serve with raw vegetables or crackers.

Nutritional Information		Diabetic Exchanges	
(per 1/4 cup serving)			
Calories	85	Vegetable	1
Fat	2 g	Medium-fat meat	1
Cholesterol	21 mg		
Sodium	323 mg		

Dill Carrot Dip

³/₄ cup reduced-calorie mayonnaise

³/₄ cup non-fat sour cream

¹/₄ cup (about one small) shredded carrot

1 tablespoon dill weed

1 tablespoon minced green onion

1 tablespoon minced parsley

1 teaspoon freshly squeezed
  lemon juice

¹/₄ teaspoon lemon pepper seasoning

¹/₄ teaspoon salt

Place ingredients in bowl and beat until well blended. Chill. Serve with vegetable sticks or crackers.

Nutritional Information		Diabetic Exchanges	
(per 1 tablespoon serving)			
Calories	30	Fat	0.5
Fat	2 g		
Cholesterol	2 mg		
Sodium	85 mg		

Apricot Prune Mui

8 ounces dark-brown sugar

4 teaspoons Hawaiian salt

1–1½ teaspoons Chinese five spice

5 whole cloves

1 cup + 2 tablespoons lemon juice

1 tablespoon + 2 teaspoons whiskey

40 ounces pitted prunes

20 ounces dried apricots

½ lemon, thinly sliced crosswise

Combine all ingredients. Let stand for two days, shaking mixture occasionally.

Nutritional Information		Diabetic Exchanges	
(per 1/4 cup serving)			
Calories	140	Fruit	2.5
Fat	0 g		
Cholesterol	0 mg		
Sodium	242 mg		

Nā lau ʻai

Salads

Broccoli-Crab Salad

Original

- 4 cups broccoli flowerettes (about 3 large stalks), parboiled for 1¹/₂ minutes
- 1 medium firm tomato, finely diced and drained well
- 1 cup sliced mushrooms
- 3 ounces imitation crab, cut into ¹/₂-inch lengths

Dressing:
- ¹/₂ cup mayonnaise
- ¹/₈ teaspoon salt
- Salt-free herb seasoning to taste

Reduced

- 4 cups broccoli flowerettes (about 3 large stalks), parboiled for 1¹/₂ minutes
- 1 medium firm tomato, finely diced and drained well
- 1 cup sliced mushrooms
- 3 ounces imitation crab, cut into ¹/₂-inch lengths

Dressing:
- ¹/₂ cup reduced-fat mayonnaise
- ¹/₈ teaspoon salt
- Salt-free herb seasoning to taste

Mix vegetables and crab in a bowl. Combine dressing ingredients; add to vegetables and mix well. Serve well-chilled.

Nutritional Information (per serving)

Original		Reduced	
Calories	170	Calories	105
Fat	15 g	Fat	7 g
Cholesterol	21 mg	Cholesterol	10 mg
Sodium	180 mg	Sodium	190 mg

Diabetic Exchanges

Original		Reduced	
Vegetable	1.0	Vegetable	1.0
Lean meat	0.5	Lean meat	0.5
Fat	2.5	Fat	1.0

Easy Crab Salad

Original

1 (16-ounce) package elbow macaroni
2 cups mayonnaise
  Salt, pepper and celery salt to taste
6 ounces imitation crab, shredded
1 stalk celery, minced
6 eggs, hard cooked
1 (10-ounce) can water chestnuts, minced
1 carrot, grated

Reduced

1 (16-ounce) package elbow macaroni
2 cups non-fat mayonnaise
  Salt, pepper and celery salt to taste
6 ounces imitation crab, shredded
1 stalk celery, minced
2 eggs, hard cooked
3 egg whites, hard cooked
1 (10-ounce) can water chestnuts, minced
1 carrot, grated

Cook elbow macaroni as directed; drain, rinse and cool. Add remaining ingredients and chill. Garnish with paprika or parsley sprigs.

Nutritional Information (per serving)				Diabetic Exchanges			
Original		Reduced		Original		Reduced	
Calories	620	Calories	275	Bread	3	Bread	3
Fat	40 g	Fat	2 g	Medium-fat meat	1	Lean meat	0.5
Cholesterol	157 mg	Cholesterol	46 mg	Fat	7		
Sodium	550 mg	Sodium	529 mg				

Nine-Layer Salad

Original

½ head lettuce, chopped
¼ cup chopped Chinese parsley
2 stalks celery, chopped
1 small Maui onion, sliced
1 medium carrot, sliced
10 ounces frozen sweet peas, thawed
2 hard cooked eggs, sliced
1 cup mayonnaise
1 teaspoon lemon juice
1 teaspoon seasoned salt
2 teaspoons milk
1 teaspoon caraway seeds (optional)
½ cup bacon bits
1 cup grated cheddar cheese

Reduced

½ head lettuce, chopped
¼ cup chopped Chinese parsley
2 stalks celery, chopped
1 small Maui onion, sliced
1 medium carrot, sliced
10 ounces frozen sweet peas, thawed
2 hard cooked eggs, sliced
1 cup reduced-calorie mayonnaise
1 teaspoon lemon juice
½ teaspoon seasoned salt
2 teaspoons skim milk
1 teaspoon caraway seeds (optional)
½ cup imitation bacon bits
1 cup grated reduced-fat cheddar cheese

Nine-Layer Salad
(continued)

Mix lettuce with Chinese parsley and place in 13 x 9-inch pan. Layer with celery, onion, carrot, peas and eggs. Mix mayonnaise, lemon juice, seasoned salt, milk and caraway seeds; spread over salad. Sprinkle with bacon bits and cheese.

Nutritional Information (per serving)

Original		Reduced	
Calories	275	Calories	180
Fat	23 g	Fat	12 g
Cholesterol	67 mg	Cholesterol	48 mg
Sodium	480 mg	Sodium	480 mg

Diabetic Exchanges

Original		Reduced	
Vegetable	2	Vegetable	2
High-fat meat	1	Medium-fat meat	1
Fat	3	Fat	1

Pasta Salad

Original

8 ounces rotini pasta (cooked, rinsed and drained)
2 cups bite-sized broccoli flowerettes
2 medium tomatoes, chopped
2 stalks green onion, chopped
1 large carrot, grated
1 small bunch parsley, finely chopped
3/4 cup Italian salad dressing

Reduced

8 ounces rotini pasta (cooked, rinsed and drained)
2 cups bite-sized broccoli flowerettes
2 medium tomatoes, chopped
2 stalks green onion, chopped
1 large carrot, grated
1 small bunch parsley, finely chopped

Dressing:
1 tablespoon wine vinegar
1/4 cup olive oil
1/2 cup low-calorie Italian salad dressing

In a large bowl, toss pasta with dressing; cover and refrigerate. Blanch broccoli in boiling water for 1 minute; drain. Add broccoli, tomato, green onion, carrot and parsley to pasta and mix well. Cover and refrigerate for at least 1 hour before serving.

Nutritional Information *(per serving)*

Original		Reduced	
Calories	180	Calories	155
Fat	11 g	Fat	6 g
Cholesterol	1 g	Cholesterol	1 g
Sodium	100 mg	Sodium	106 mg

Diabetic Exchanges

Original		Reduced	
Vegetable	1	Vegetable	1
Bread	1	Bread	1
Fat	2	Fat	1

Asian Seafood Salad

Serves 10

2 tablespoons grated ginger
2 tablespoons minced garlic
2 onions, julienned
1 tablespoon minced lemon grass
1 tablespoon peanut oil
2 red bell peppers, julienned
4 cups broccoli flowerettes
1 carrot, julienned
1 pound scallops
1 pound shrimp (16–20 per pound)
1 pound kai choy, shredded

1 pound bok choy, shredded
2 tablespoons fresh basil, shredded
1/4 cup minced Chinese parsley
2 tablespoons chopped mint
2 tablespoons sesame oil
2 tablespoons lime juice
2–3 Hawaiian chili peppers, minced, OR
1 teaspoon sambal (Indonesian chili paste)
5 cups cooked buckwheat (soba) noodles (8 ounces uncooked)

Sauté ginger, garlic, onion and lemon grass in a large pot or wok in peanut oil for 2 to 3 minutes. Add peppers, broccoli and carrot; sauté for 2 minutes. Add scallops, shrimp, cabbages, basil, Chinese parsley, mint, sesame oil, lime juice and chili peppers or sambal. Cover and steam 4 to 6 minutes until seafood is lightly cooked. Chill. Garnish with green onion and lemon wedges. Serve with soba.

Nutritional Information

(per serving)

Calories	230
Fat	6 g
Cholesterol	88 mg
Sodium	379 mg

Diabetic Exchanges

Vegetable	1.5
Bread	1.0
Lean meat	2.0

Warm Ahi Salad

Vinaigrette:

1 tablespoon minced shallot

$1/2$ teaspoon minced fresh thyme
  (or $1/4$ teaspoon dried)

$1/2$ teaspoon minced fresh tarragon
  (or $1/4$ teaspoon dried)

1 tablespoon extra-virgin olive oil
  (or 1 tablespoon toasted sesame oil)

2 tablespoons + 1 teaspoon sherry wine vinegar or
  red wine vinegar

1 large Belgian endive, separated into leaves

3 cups torn mixed greens (curly endive,
  radicchio, red lettuce, romaine, etc.)

1 cup shredded mixed colored raw vegetables (red
  cabbage, carrot, red or yellow peppers, etc.)

8 ounces ahi steak, 1 to $1^{1}/2$ inches thick, cut in half

2 teaspoons low-sodium shoyu
  Salt and freshly ground pepper to taste

$1/4$ teaspoon black sesame seed

Preheat broiler or grill. To make vinaigrette, whisk first five ingredients together in a small bowl and set aside. Arrange Belgian endive on two plates in a spoke pattern. Top with tossed mixed raw vegetables. Lightly brush ahi steaks with shoyu; salt and pepper both sides. Broil or grill ahi 6 inches from heat until just barely cooked and still pink in center, about 4 minutes per side. Slice ahi on diagonal and place in spoke pattern on top of salad greens. Drizzle with vinaigrette and sprinkle with black sesame seed.

Nutritional Information		Diabetic Exchanges	
(per serving)			
Calories	215	Vegetable	2
Fat	8 g	Lean meat	3
Cholesterol	51 mg		
Sodium	366 mg		

Thai-Style Chicken Salad

 1 pound boneless, skinless chicken breast
   Salt and pepper
15 leaves Manoa lettuce, torn
15 leaves red leaf lettuce, torn
20 sprigs watercress
10 leaves endive
10 stalks green onion, chopped
1¼ cups cucumber sliced thinly
 5 medium shallots, sliced
 1 tomato, peeled, seeded and cut into strips
10 ounces bean sprouts
2½ cups shredded green papaya

20 sprigs Chinese parsley
25 mint leaves

Dressing:

1½ stalks lemon grass, minced
 3 tablespoons fish sauce
 5 tablespoons lime juice
 2 tablespoons chopped mint
 2 tablespoons honey
 3 teaspoons minced garlic
 2 tablespoons peanut oil
 1 teaspoon Thai chili sauce (or to taste)

Season chicken with salt and pepper to taste and steam, being careful not to overcook. Set aside to cool, then slice thin. Combine dressing ingredients and toss with vegetables (except Chinese parsley and mint), chicken and papaya. Adjust seasoning, if desired. Place in serving bowls and garnish with Chinese parsley and mint.

Nutritional Information

(per serving)

Calories	285
Fat	9 g
Cholesterol	60 mg
Sodium	760 mg

Diabetic Exchanges

Vegetable	2
Lean meat	3
Fruit	1

Tofu-Tuna-Tomato Salad

1 large block tofu, drained and cut into small cubes
1 (6$1/2$-ounce) can water-packed tuna, drained
1 large tomato, diced
1 small Maui onion, chopped
$1/2$ cup chopped green onion
1 head red leaf lettuce, torn

Dressing:
1 tablespoon sesame oil
3 tablespoons low-sodium shoyu
3 tablespoons rice vinegar
3 teaspoons sugar
$1/4$ teaspoon garlic powder

Place lettuce in large salad bowl or on platter. Top with tofu, tuna, tomato and onion. Combine dressing ingredients and mix well; pour over salad just before serving.

Nutritional Information
(per serving)

Calories	170
Fat	7 g
Cholesterol	16 mg
Sodium	330 mg

Diabetic Exchanges

Vegetable	2
Lean meat	2

Spicy Shrimp Salad
with Cool Mango Dressing

1 medium mango
2 tablespoons lemon juice
1 pound large shrimp, peeled and deveined
1 tablespoon chicken stock
2 teaspoon chili powder
1/2 teaspoon liquid hot pepper sauce (more, if desired)

1 1/2 cups pineapple, chopped and drained well
1 cup chopped tomatoes
1 medium red onion, thinly sliced
2 cups torn greens

Peel mango and cut flesh away from the seed. In a blender or food processor, puree mango and lemon juice. In a large non-stick frying pan, cook shrimp, stock, chili powder and hot pepper sauce over medium-high heat until shrimp are cooked through, about 3 minutes. Remove from heat, drain and chill. Add pineapple, tomatoes and onion. Line a large platter with the greens, spoon the shrimp mixture over. Drizzle with mango puree.

Nutritional Information

(per serving)

Calories	205
Fat	3 g
Cholesterol	172 mg
Sodium	176 mg

Diabetic Exchanges

Fruit	1.5
Lean meat	2.0

Won Bok Chicken Salad

8 ounces noodles (somen, look fun or spaghetti)

4 cups shredded won bok (Chinese) cabbage

1 pound cooked boneless, skinless chicken breast, cubed

$1/4$ cup minced green onion

$1/2$ teaspoon salt (optional)

$1/4$ teaspoon pepper

1 teaspoon sesame seed, crushed

   Crushed garlic and grated ginger to taste

3–4 tablespoons lemon or lime juice
   (grated rind optional)

Cook noodles as directed, then drain and place on serving platter. Combine salt, pepper, sesame seed, garlic, ginger and lemon or lime juice; mix and add to noodles. Add chicken, won bok and green onion; toss gently. May be served as is, chilled, steamed or microwaved.

Nutritional Information		Diabetic Exchanges	
(per serving)			
Calories	300	Bread	2
Fat	8 g	Lean meat	3
Cholesterol	103 mg		
Sodium	256 mg		

Green Papaya Salad

¹/₂ pound green papaya (1 large fruit)

2–3 red chili peppers, seeded

1 clove garlic

1 tomato, sliced in strips

3 tablespoons lime juice

3 tablespoons fish sauce

¹/₂ cup ground peanuts

Salted shrimp powder and sugar to taste

1 lime, cut in wedges

Lettuce or cabbage leaves

Peel and seed papaya, then grate. Grind together red chili peppers and garlic in food processor or mortar. Mix together papaya, tomato, lime juice and fish sauce. Add garlic mixture and toss lightly. Place portion of papaya mixture onto lettuce or cabbage leaf. Sprinkle with ground peanuts, salted shrimp powder and a dash of sugar. Fold into a packet to eat. Serve with wedges of lime. Garnish with chili peppers and crushed peanuts.

Nutritional Information		Diabetic Exchanges	
(per serving)			
Calories	100	Vegetable	1.0
Fat	4 g	Fruit	0.5
Cholesterol	0 mg	Fat	1.0
Sodium	443 mg		

Three-Bean Salad

¼ cup apple cider vinegar

2 tablespoons honey

¼ cup water

2 tablespoons frozen apple juice concentrate

1 cup fresh green beans, steamed and cut into ½-inch pieces, or canned green beans, rinsed and drained

1 cup cooked or canned garbanzo beans, rinsed and drained

1 cup cooked or canned kidney beans, rinsed and drained

¼ cup sliced red onion

Prepare dressing by whisking vinegar, honey, water and apple juice concentrate together until well blended. Combine beans and onion in a bowl. Pour dressing over beans and mix well. Cover and let marinate at room temperature at least 30 minutes. Chill at least 30 minutes and toss again before serving.

Nutritional Information		Diabetic Exchanges	
(per serving)			
Calories	185	Bread	2
Fat	1 g	Vegetable	1
Cholesterol	0 mg		
Sodium	10 mg		

Marinated Eggplant Salad

2 pounds Japanese eggplant

3 cloves garlic

2 tablespoons balsamic or red wine vinegar

2 tablespoons fresh lemon juice

1 tablespoon olive oil

3 tablespoons fresh rosemary, chopped, or
   1$\frac{1}{2}$ tablespoons dried

   Salt and pepper

2 bunches spinach, cleaned and stemmed

5 plum tomatoes or 3 round tomatoes, seeded
   and chopped

Slice eggplant $\frac{1}{4}$-inch thick and place in colander. Sprinkle with salt and let stand for 45 minutes. Rinse and pat dry. In a large mixing bowl, combine garlic, vinegar, lemon juice, olive oil and rosemary. In a non-stick skillet coated with non-stick cooking spray, sauté eggplant until tender, about 15 minutes. (If you don't have a non-stick skillet, sauté in $\frac{1}{4}$ cup vegetable stock.) Chill eggplant, then add to the ingredients in the mixing bowl. Toss with spinach then top with tomatoes and serve. Drizzle with any leftover marinade.

Nutritional Information		Diabetic Exchanges	
(per serving)			
Calories	60	Vegetable	2
Fat	2 g		
Cholesterol	0 mg		
Sodium	10 mg		

Spinach Salad

1 bunch fresh spinach
¼ teaspoon salt
2 teaspoons sesame oil
2 stalks green onion, trimmed and chopped
1 clove garlic, minced

Wash spinach and steam just until tender. Drain and squeeze out as much water as possible. Chop coarsely. Combine salt, sesame oil, green onion and garlic. Mix into spinach.

Nutritional Information		Diabetic Exchanges	
(per serving)			
Calories	35	Vegetable	0.5
Fat	3 g	Fat	0.5
Cholesterol	0 mg		
Sodium	178 mg		

Yellow Bean Sprout Salad

1 pound bean sprouts

½ cup water

½ teaspoon hot red pepper

2 stalks green onion, chopped

2 cloves garlic, minced

1½ teaspoons sesame oil

1½ teaspoons salt

Wash bean sprouts and place in a pot with water. Bring slowly to a boil. Cover tightly and steam for 10 minutes. Drain immediately. Add remaining ingredients and mix well. Serve hot or cold.

Nutritional Information		*Diabetic Exchanges*	
(per serving)			
Calories	35	Vegetable	1
Fat	1 g		
Cholesterol	0 mg		
Sodium	538 mg		

Miso-Su Salad Dressing

¹/₃ cup miso
1 tablespoon vinegar
¹/₄ cup apple juice
1 tablespoon sugar or honey
1 small clove garlic, crushed
1 teaspoon grated ginger

Mix all ingredients together. Adjust ingredients to taste.

Nutritional Information		Diabetic Exchanges	
(per 2 tablespoon serving)			
Calories	45	Bread	0.5
Fat	1 g		
Cholesterol	0 mg		
Sodium	550 mg		

Papaya Seed Salad Dressing

1 medium papaya
$^1/_3$ cup cold water
1 1-inch piece kanten (agar agar) or 2 teaspoons
  unflavored gelatin
  (use less if thinner consistency is desired)
1 tablespoon vegetable oil
$^1/_3$ cup apple juice
1 tablespoon lime or lemon juice

$^1/_4$ cup red wine vinegar or rice
  vinegar
$^1/_4$ cup sugar or honey
$^1/_2$ teaspoon paprika
1–2 teaspoon Worcestershire sauce
$^1/_2$ teaspoon dry mustard
1 large clove garlic
  Small piece onion

Cut papaya in half and remove seeds, reserving 1$^1/_2$ tablespoons. Dissolve kanten or gelatin in cold water; heat in microwave until completely smooth. Place seeds in food processor or blender and process until the size of coarsely ground pepper. Add oil, juices, vinegar and seasonings and blend. Slowly add gelatin to mixture. Serve with papaya and salad greens.

Nutritional Information

(per 2 tablespoon serving)

Calories	30
Fat	1 g
Cholesterol	0 mg
Sodium	6 mg

Diabetic Exchanges

Fruit	0.5

Nā kupa

Soups

Portuguese Bean Soup

Original

2 cups (1 pound) dried red or pink beans OR
  2 (15-ounce) cans red or pink beans, drained
  and rinsed

2¹/₂–5 quarts water

2 pounds Portuguese sausage

1 onion, sliced

3 carrots, sliced

3 medium baking potatoes, diced

3 stalks celery, sliced

1 small head cabbage (about 1 pound), chopped

1 (8-ounce) can tomato sauce

¹/₂ cup ketchup

1 tablespoon salt

1 clove garlic, minced

1 cup uncooked macaroni

Reduced

2 cups (1 pound) dried red or pink beans OR
  2 (15-ounce) cans red or pink beans, drained
  and rinsed

2¹/₂–5 quarts water

¹/₄ pound turkey ham

¹/₂ pound Portuguese sausage

1 large onion, sliced

3 carrots, diced or sliced

3 medium baking potatoes, diced

3 stalks celery, sliced

1 small head cabbage (about 1 pound), chopped

1 (8-ounce) can no-salt-added tomato sauce

¹/₂ cup ketchup

¹/₂ teaspoon Portuguese spice*

3 tablespoons minced parsley

1 clove garlic, minced

1 cup uncooked macaroni

Portuguese Bean Soup
(continued)

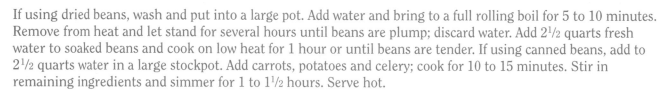

If using dried beans, wash and put into a large pot. Add water and bring to a full rolling boil for 5 to 10 minutes. Remove from heat and let stand for several hours until beans are plump; discard water. Add 2½ quarts fresh water to soaked beans and cook on low heat for 1 hour or until beans are tender. If using canned beans, add to 2½ quarts water in a large stockpot. Add carrots, potatoes and celery; cook for 10 to 15 minutes. Stir in remaining ingredients and simmer for 1 to 1½ hours. Serve hot.

*Portuguese Spice
Mix equal portions of anise seed, cinnamon sticks, whole cloves, black peppercorns and whole allspice. Warm in oven at 250 degrees for 20 minutes, then grind in blender, food processor or coffee/spice grinder until fine.

Nutritional Information (per 2 cup serving)   Diabetic Exchanges

Original		Reduced		Original		Reduced	
Calories	515	Calories	300	Vegetable	1	Bread	3
Fat	27 g	Fat	7 g	Bread	3	Medium-fat meat	1
Cholesterol	62 mg	Cholesterol	21 mg	Medium-fat meat	2		
Sodium	1,777 mg	Sodium	485mg	Fat	3		

Oriental Split Pea Soup

1 ounce dried shiitake mushrooms (4-5 pieces) soaked in 1 cup water (reserve water)

1 medium onion, thinly sliced

1½ cups diagonally sliced celery

¾ pound boneless, skinless chicken breast

7 (14-ounce) cans defatted, reduced-sodium chicken broth

5½ cups water

1 pound dried green split peas

2 tablespoons grated ginger

2 cups peeled and diced carrots

1 bunch watercress, washed and chopped

1 teaspoon chili sesame oil

Remove mushroom stems and discard; dice caps and set aside. Place mushroom water, onion, celery, chicken, broth and water in a large stockpot. Bring to a boil, then reduce heat and simmer for 40 minutes. Remove chicken and set aside. Wash split peas; add to pot with ginger, carrots and mushrooms. Bring to a boil and simmer for 1½ hours. Dice chicken and return to pot with watercress and chili oil. Simmer for ½ hour or until split peas are tender. Serve hot.

Nutritional Information

(per 1 cup serving)

Calories	270
Fat	2 g
Cholesterol	24 mg
Sodium	343 mg

Diabetic Exchanges

Bread	2
Lean meat	2

Pasta and Bean Soup

1¹/₂ cups uncooked elbow or shell macaroni
   Non-stick cooking spray
1 large onion, chopped
3 stalks celery, sliced
3 carrots, chopped
1 (15-ounce) can no-salt-added stewed tomatoes, undrained
1 (14-ounce) can defatted, reduced-sodium chicken broth

2 cups water
¹/₂ teaspoon black pepper
¹/₈ teaspoon chili powder (optional)
¹/₂ teaspoon dried parsley flakes
1 (15-ounce) can red kidney beans, drained and rinsed
1 (15-ounce) can white beans, drained and rinsed

Cook macaroni in unsalted water until tender; drain, rinse and set aside. Coat bottom of a large stockpot with non-stick cooking spray; sauté onion, celery and carrots until tender. Add tomatoes with liquid, broth water and seasonings; heat to boiling. Reduce heat to low; simmer, uncovered, for 30 minutes. Stir in macaroni and beans; heat through and serve.

Nutritional Information		Diabetic Exchanges	
(per 1 cup serving)			
Calories	250	Bread	3
Fat	1 g		
Cholesterol	0 mg		
Sodium	160 mg		

Black Bean Soup

2 (15-ounce) cans black beans, drained and rinsed

4 cups water

2 medium Maui onions, chopped

3 cloves garlic, crushed

2 teaspoons chili powder

1/2 teaspoon cumin

1/2 teaspoon salt

1/8 teaspoon nutmeg

Cayenne pepper or liquid hot pepper sauce to taste

Garnish:

1/2 cup reduced-fat sour cream or plain yogurt, chili powder, sliced green onion and chopped Chinese parsley

Combine beans, water, onion, garlic and spices in a large stockpot; simmer for 30 minutes. Remove 3 cups of soup and puree in blender. Return puree to pot, adjusting seasonings as desired. Simmer 10 to 15 minutes. Ladle into bowls and garnish with a dollop of sour cream or yogurt, a dash of chili powder, and green onion and Chinese parsley.

Nutritional Information		Diabetic Exchanges	
(per 1 cup serving)			
Calories	190	Bread	2.0
Fat	1 g	Lean meat	0.5
Cholesterol	2 mg		
Sodium	204 mg		

Minestrone Soup

1 (15-ounce) can navy or kidney beans, drained and rinsed

1 (14-ounce) can defatted, reduced-sodium chicken broth

1 quart water

2 medium carrots, diced

1/2 small head cabbage, shredded

1 medium potato, diced

1 (15-ounce) can no-salt-added tomatoes, undrained
Non-stick cooking spray

1 medium onion, sliced

2 stalks celery, sliced diagonally

1 medium zucchini, sliced

2 cloves garlic, minced

1/8 teaspoon black pepper

1 teaspoon dried basil

1/4 teaspoon dried (or 1/8 teaspoon ground) marjoram

2 tablespoons chopped parsley

1 (8-ounce) can no-salt-added tomato sauce

1/2 cup uncooked macaroni

In a large stockpot (6–8 quart) add beans, carrots, cabbage, potatoes and tomatoes to chicken broth and water. Cook for 30 minutes. Coat bottom of small skillet with non-stick cooking spray; sauté onion for a few minutes. Add celery, zucchini, garlic, pepper, basil and marjoram; continue to sauté until vegetables are crisp-tender. Add to beans and vegetable mixture with parsley, tomato sauce and noodles. Cook for 20 minutes or until macaroni is tender. Add more water if too thick. Serve hot.

Nutritional Information

(per 1 cup serving)

Calories	105
Fat	0 g
Cholesterol	0 mg
Sodium	114 mg

Diabetic Exchanges

Vegetable	1
Bread	1

Creamy Carrot Soup

Non-stick cooking spray
1/2 cup chopped onion
2 cloves garlic, minced
3 cups water
4 cups carrots, thinly sliced crosswise
2 tablespoons light-brown sugar

1 packet low-sodium vegetable or
   chicken boullion granules
2 teaspoons curry powder
1/8 teaspoon ground ginger
   Dash of cinnamon
1/2 cup skim milk

Coat the bottom of a small skillet with non-stick cooking spray. Sauté onion and garlic until tender. In a large saucepan, bring water to a boil. Add remaining ingredients except milk. Reduce heat and simmer covered for 40 minutes or until carrots are tender. Remove from heat and pour mixture in batches into food processor or blender. Puree until smooth and return to saucepan. Reduce heat to low and stir in milk, heating until warm but not boiling. Serve warm.

Nutritional Information

(per 1 cup serving)

Calories	120
Fat	1 g
Cholesterol	1 mg
Sodium	182 mg

Diabetic Exchanges

Vegetable	2
Bread	1

Chinese Cabbage Soup

3 cups defatted, reduced-sodium chicken or beef broth

1 tablespoon low-sodium shoyu

1½ tablespoons sake or white wine

½ teaspoon sugar

⅛ teaspoon Chinese five spice, or to taste

⅛ teaspoon pepper, or to taste

½ pound Chinese cabbage, chopped into 1-inch pieces

2 dried shiitake mushrooms, soaked in water and sliced OR
¼ cup fresh mushrooms, sliced

2 tablespoons chopped Chinese parsley

3 tablespoons chopped green onion

6 ounces firm tofu, cut into cubes

Garnish:
Chinese parsley and green onion

In a stockpot, heat broth, shoyu, sake, sugar, Chinese five spice and pepper to boiling. Add cabbage, mushrooms, Chinese parsley and green onion to boiling soup; cook uncovered until cabbage is crisp-tender. Stir in tofu and heat to boiling. Garnish and serve hot.

Nutritional Information		Diabetic Exchanges	
(per 1 cup serving)			
Calories	55	Vegetable	1.0
Fat	2 g	Lean meat	0.5
Cholesterol	1 mg		
Sodium	448 mg		

Spinach and Noodle Soup

2 quarts defatted, reduced-sodium chicken broth

1 pound fresh or ¼ pound dried thin or medium Asian egg, wheat or buckwheat (soba) noodles

1½ cups packed fresh spinach leaves, washed, trimmed and cut crosswise into ¼- to ½-inch wide strips

2 tablespoons low-sodium shoyu

¼ cup chopped green onion

Place broth in a large saucepan and bring to a boil over high heat. Cover and reduce heat to low. In another large saucepan, bring unsalted water to a boil and cook noodles until tender. Drain, rinse briefly under cold water, drain again, then toss gently with spinach. Divide noodle-spinach mixture among eight soup bowls. Stir shoyu into warm broth and ladle into bowls. Garnish with green onion.

Nutritional Information

(per 1 cup serving)

Calories	200
Fat	1 g
Cholesterol	0 mg
Sodium	387 mg

Diabetic Exchanges

Vegetable	1
Bread	2

Fresh Mushroom Soup

1 pound fresh mushrooms, coarsely chopped
   Non-stick cooking spray
2 cups water
2 cups non-fat dry milk
1 teaspoon dried onion flakes

1 tablespoon dried parsley flakes
2 tablespoons all-purpose flour
1 tablespoon sherry
¼ teaspoon salt, or to taste
   Freshly ground black pepper to taste

Coat a heavy saucepan with non-stick cooking spray. Heat saucepan and sauté mushrooms quickly just until crisp-tender; set aside. Combine remaining ingredients in a blender and process until thick and foamy. Add mushrooms and blend again at lowest speed for 4 to 5 seconds or until mushrooms are chopped into fine pieces but not pulverized. Return mixture to saucepan and heat gently, stirring with a wire whisk to prevent scorching.

Nutritional Information

(per 1 cup serving)

Calories	130
Fat	1 g
Cholesterol	5 mg
Sodium	269 mg

Diabetic Exchanges

Vegetable	1
Skim milk	1

Egg Drop Soup

½ cup slivered bamboo shoots

1 ounce dried shiitake mushrooms (4-5 pieces) soaked in 1 cup water (reserve water)

¼ cup frozen peas (do not thaw)

4 thin slices ginger, crushed

Pepper to taste

7 packages low-sodium chicken bouillon granules dissolved in 7 cups water, divided

2 tablespoons cornstarch

1 egg

1 tablespoon water

Low-sodium shoyu to taste (optional)

In a medium saucepan, combine bamboo shoots, mushrooms with reserved water, frozen peas, ginger, pepper and 6¾ cups chicken broth. Bring to a boil. In a small bowl, mix remaining ¼ cup broth with cornstarch until well blended. Add to vegetable mixture and cook, stirring occasionally, for about 5 minutes. Beat egg and water in a small bowl; pour into soup slowly, stirring slightly with a fork to form threads. Cook about 1 minute; serve hot.

Nutritional Information

(per 1 cup serving)

Calories	30
Fat	1 g
Cholesterol	26 mg
Sodium	31 mg

Diabetic Exchanges

Vegetable	1

Corn and Pepper Chowder

Non-stick cooking spray
1 cup chopped onion
1 cup diced red bell pepper
2½ tablespoons all-purpose flour
½ teaspoon cumin
⅛ teaspoon cayenne pepper
2 cups water
1¼ cups peeled and diced potato

1 packet low-sodium chicken-flavored
  bouillon granules
¼ pound lean roasted ham
2 cups frozen whole-kernel corn
2 tablespoons canned chopped green chilies, drained
1 cup evaporated skim milk
¼ teaspoon black pepper

Coat a large stockpot with non-stick cooking spray. Place over medium-high heat until hot; sauté onion and bell pepper for 5 minutes or until tender. Stir in flour, cumin and cayenne pepper; cook 1 minute, stirring constantly. Gradually stir in water, then add potato, bouillon and ham. Bring to a boil, stirring frequently. Cover, reduce heat and simmer 10 minutes or until potatoes are tender and mixture is thickened. Add corn, chilies, milk and pepper; heat through, stirring occasionally.

Nutritional Information

(per 1 cup serving)

Calories	180
Fat	2 g
Cholesterol	12 mg
Sodium	308 mg

Diabetic Exchanges

Bread	2.0
Lean meat	0.5

Fishcake Miso Soup

1/4 cup white miso

1/2 pound raw Chinese fishcake

2 tablespoons finely diced carrots

1 tablespoon minced green onion

5 cups water

1 tablespoon sake

2 tablespoons hondashi or other flavored soup stock

1/2 cup tofu, cubed

Garnish:

Green onion and wakame (seaweed)

Mix miso with 2 tablespoons water; set aside. In a small bowl, mix fishcake, carrots and green onion. Bring water to a boil in a large pot. Using a wet teaspoon, drop fishcake mixture into the hot water. Add prepared miso mixture, sake, hondashi and tofu. Simmer 7 minutes or until done. Garnish, if desired; serve hot.

Note: Use two packets low-sodium bouillion granules to reduce sodium content.

Nutritional Information		Diabetic Exchanges	
(per 1 cup serving)			
Calories	100	Vegetable	1.5
Fat	3 g	Lean meat	1.0
Cholesterol	7 mg		
Sodium	758 mg		

Shrimp and Fish Soup

Non-stick cooking spray

2 teaspoons vegetable oil

1 cup chopped green bell pepper

1/2 cup chopped onion

1 clove garlic, minced

1 tablespoon all-purpose flour

2 1/2 cups water

1 1/2 cups peeled and diced potato

1/2 cup frozen whole-kernel corn (do not thaw)

1 teaspoon dried thyme

1/4 teaspoon salt

1/4 teaspoon cayenne pepper

1 (15-ounce) can no-salt-added chopped tomatoes, undrained

1/2 pound mahimahi or other white fish fillets, cut into 1-inch pieces

1 pound fresh medium-sized shrimp, peeled and deveined

Coat a large stockpot with non-stick cooking spray; add oil and place over medium heat until hot. Add bell pepper, onion and garlic; sauté until crisp-tender. Sprinkle with flour; stir well and cook 1 minute. Stir in water, potato, corn, thyme, salt, cayenne pepper and tomatoes. Bring to a boil, then reduce heat and simmer uncovered for 30 minutes or until potato is tender. Add shrimp and fish; stir well. Increase heat to medium; cover and cook 5 minutes or until seafood is done.

Nutritional Information		Diabetic Exchanges	
(per 1 cup serving)			
Calories	170	Bread	1
Fat	3 g	Lean meat	2
Cholesterol	127 mg		
Sodium	221 mg		

Fish Sabaw

4 cups water
1 stalk lemon grass, sliced
1 medium onion, chopped
1 large potato, cubed
1 1-inch piece ginger, crushed
1 teaspoon patis (Filipino fish sauce), optional
½ teaspoon Hawaiian salt

½ pound akule, opelu (jack fish)
   or any fresh island fish
¼ cup lime juice

Garnish:
1 bunch green onion, marungay leaves, chili pepper
   leaves or spinach leaves
Liquid hot pepper sauce to taste

Boil lemon grass in water about 15 minutes; remove and discard lemon grass. Add onion, potato and ginger to water; return to boiling. Reduce heat to low and simmer until vegetables are tender. Stir in patis, salt and fish. Cook on medium heat until fish is done; reduce heat and simmer 2 minutes. Remove from heat and add lime juice. Garnish and serve hot.

Nutritional Information		Diabetic Exchanges	
(per 1 cup serving)			
Calories	150	Vegetable	0.5
Fat	1 g	Bread	0.5
Cholesterol	25 mg	Lean meat	2.0
Sodium	258 mg		

Mundoo Soup

1½ cups tofu

2 cups coarsely chopped cabbage

12 ounces bean sprouts, washed and drained

½ pound lean ground beef

2 tablespoons minced onion

1 1-inch piece ginger, minced

3 tablespoons minced green onion

3 cloves garlic, minced

1½ tablespoons low-sodium shoyu

1½ teaspoons sesame oil

50 mundoo wrappers

9 (14-ounce cans) defatted, reduced-sodium chicken broth

Garnish:

2–3 tablespoons minced green onion

Press excess water out of tofu. In a large stockpot, cook cabbage and bean sprouts in water to cover; drain and squeeze. Finely chop tofu, cabbage and bean sprouts. Combine all ingredients except mundoo wrappers and broth in a mixing bowl. Place 1 tablespoon filling in the center of each wrapper, fold into half-moon shape and seal edges with water. Steam for about 15 minutes or until meat is done. Serve mundoo in hot chicken broth, garnished with chopped green onions.

Note: To reduce sodium content, use 16 packages low-sodium bouillion granules dissolved in 16 cups water.

Nutritional Information		Diabetic Exchanges	
(per 1 cup, 3 piece serving)			
Calories	90	Bread	1.0
Fat	3 g	Lean meat	0.5
Sodium	738 mg		

Beef Barley Soup

Non-stick cooking spray
3/4 pound center-cut beef shank, visible fat removed
2 quarts water
1 medium onion, peeled and quartered
1 bay leaf
1/2 teaspoon salt

Freshly ground black pepper to taste
3 cups peeled and diced potatoes
1 cup thickly sliced celery
1 1/4 cups diced carrots
3 tablespoons uncooked pearl barley
2 teaspoons thyme

Preheat broiler. Lightly coat broiler pan with non-stick cooking spray. Broil meat for 5 minutes on each side or until thoroughly browned. In a large stockpot, combine meat, water, onion, bay leaf, salt and pepper. Bring to a boil, then reduce heat and simmer for 3 hours or until meat is tender. Remove meat and set aside. Strain broth, chill in freezer, then skim off fat. Cut meat into bite-sized pieces. Place broth, meat and remaining ingredients in stockpot and bring to a boil. Reduce heat and simmer 20 minutes or until vegetables are tender. Serve hot.

Nutritional Information		Diabetic Exchanges	
(per 1 cup serving)			
Calories	140	Bread	1
Fat	3 g	Lean meat	1
Cholesterol	37 mg		
Sodium	206 mg		

Nā pūpū

Side Dishes

Chow Fun

Original

½ pound pork, chopped

¼ pound ham, cut in strips

2 cups bean sprouts

2 stalks celery, sliced diagonally

1 cup string beans

2 stalks green onion, cut into ½-inch pieces

1 1-inch piece ginger, crushed

2 teaspoons salt

½ teaspoon sugar

2 eggs

3 pounds look fun noodles, cut in ½–¾-inch slices

2 tablespoons each sesame seeds, oil and shoyu

Reduced

2 teaspoons sesame oil

½ pound boneless, skinless chicken

2 cloves garlic, minced

1 small onion, thinly sliced

1 1-inch piece ginger, crushed

1 (12-ounce) package bean sprouts

½ cup julienned carrot

½ cup julienned celery

1 tablespoon oyster sauce

Pepper to taste

2 pounds look fun noodles, cut in ½–¾-inch slices

2 stalks green onion, cut into ½-inch pieces

Heat sesame oil in large skillet or wok. Stir-fry chicken, garlic, onion and ginger; add bean sprouts, carrot and celery. Add oyster sauce, pepper, look fun and green onion. Cook for about a minute, or until hot. Garnish with 2 tablespoons toasted sesame seeds and Chinese parsley.

Nutritional Information (per serving)

Original		Reduced	
Calories	400	Calories	245
Fat	13 g	Fat	5 g
Cholesterol	143 mg	Cholesterol	25 mg
Sodium	1028 mg	Sodium	40 mg

Diabetic Exchanges

Original		Reduced	
Bread	3	Bread	2.0
Medium-fat meat	2	Lean meat	1.5
Fat	1		

Chinese Taro Cake

Original

2	cups diced taro
1¼	cups water
1	cup all-purpose flour
1	teaspoon salt
¾	cup diced char siu
½	cup soaked dried shrimp, finely diced
¼	cup diced ham
½	cup chopped green onion
2	tablespoons chopped Chinese parsley
2	tablespoons chopped chung choi (preserved cabbage)
2	eggs
1–2	teaspoons sesame seeds

Reduced

	Non-stick cooking spray
2	cups diced taro
1¼	cups water
1	cup all-purpose flour
½	teaspoon salt
½	cup diced char siu, fat removed
½	cup diced turkey ham
¼	cup soaked dried shrimp, finely diced
½	cup chopped green onion
2	tablespoons chopped Chinese parsley
2	tablespoons chopped chung choi (preserved cabbage)
1	egg
2	egg whites
1–2	teaspoons sesame seeds

Chinese Taro Cake
(continued)

Coat two 9-inch pans (round or square) with non-stick cooking spray. Combine all ingredients except egg, egg whites and sesame seeds. Turn into pans and cover with aluminum foil. Bake at 300 degrees for 1 hour, 15 minutes. Uncover and cool. Beat egg and egg whites together. Coat a skillet with non-stick cooking spray. Pour eggs into a thin sheet and cook slowly, turning once. Slice into thin strips. Cut taro cakes into diamonds; garnish with egg strips and sesame seeds.

Nutritional Information (per 2 piece serving)   Diabetic Exchanges

Original		Reduced		Original		Reduced	
Calories	141	Calories	115	Bread	1	Bread	1
Fat	5 g	Fat	3 g	Medium-fat meat	1	Lean meat	1
Cholesterol	78 mg	Cholesterol	39 mg				
Sodium	277 mg	Sodium	271 mg				

Chow Mein

Original

¹/₂ pound chow mein noodles

3 tablespoons vegetable oil

1 pound boneless lean steak, chicken or shelled shrimp

3 tablespoons cornstarch

3 cups beef or chicken broth

2 teaspoons sugar

1 teaspoon monosodium glutamate

1 teaspoon salt

¹/₄ teaspoon black pepper

2 tablespoons shoyu

1 pound chop suey vegetables

Reduced

8 ounces chow mein noodles
Non-stick cooking spray

¹/₄ pound lean pork cutlet

1 teaspoon vegetable oil

1 clove garlic, minced

1 teaspoon sugar

¹/₄ teaspoon black pepper

2 tablespoons low-sodium shoyu

3 cups defatted, reduced-sodium chicken, beef or pork stock, divided

1 pound chop suey vegetables

3 tablespoons cornstarch

Chow Mein
(continued)

Cook noodles in boiling, unsalted water for 3 to 5 minutes. Drain and rinse with cold water; set aside.
Sauté pork in a skillet coated with non-stick cooking spray; remove and set aside. Add oil and noodles to skillet; stir-fry for about 2 minutes. Place noodles on platter and keep warm. Return pork to skillet with garlic, sugar, pepper, shoyu and 1 cup broth. Bring to a boil; add vegetables and cook for 1 to 2 minutes or until crisp-tender. Mix remaining broth with cornstarch; stir into vegetables and cook until thickened. Pour vegetables and gravy over noodles. Serve hot.

Nutritional Information (per serving)

Original		Reduced	
Calories	335	Calories	195
Fat	24 g	Fat	5 g
Cholesterol	55 mg	Cholesterol	11 mg
Sodium	1475 mg	Sodium	961 mg

Diabetic Exchanges

Original		Reduced	
Vegetable	2	Vegetable	2
Bread	2	Bread	1
Medium fat-meat	2	Medium fat-meat	1
Fat	2		

Cornbread

Original

- ½ cup all-purpose flour
- 1½ cups cornmeal
- 2 tablespoons sugar
- 2 teaspoons baking powder
- 1 teaspoon salt
- 2 eggs
- 1½ cups buttermilk
- ¼ cup vegetable oil

Reduced

- 1 cup all-purpose flour
- ¾ cup cornmeal
- 1 tablespoon sugar
- 1 tablespoon baking powder
- ½ teaspoon salt
- 2 egg whites
- 1 cup skim milk
- 1 tablespoon vegetable oil
- Non-stick cooking spray

Preheat oven to 400 degrees. In a medium mixing bowl, stir together flour, cornmeal, sugar, baking powder and salt; set aside. In a small mixing bowl, beat egg whites, milk and oil. Stir into dry ingredients just until mixed. Pour batter into a 9-inch square baking pan coated with non-stick cooking spray. Bake for 20 to 25 minutes or until a toothpick inserted near center comes out clean.

Note: Stir one 4-ounce can chopped green chilies, drained, into wet ingredients.

Nutritional Information (per serving)				Diabetic Exchanges			
Original		Reduced		Original		Reduced	
Calories	155	Calories	95	Bread	1.5	Bread	1
Fat	6 g	Fat	2 g	Fat	1.0		
Cholesterol	36 mg	Cholesterol	0 mg				
Sodium	276 mg	Sodium	183 mg				

Cucumber Namasu

1   cucumber
1   tablespoon chopped onion
1   tablespoon chopped celery
1–2 teaspoons grated ginger
2–3 tablespoons sugar
2–3 tablespoons vinegar
2–3 tablespoons lemon juice

Peel cucumber, leaving alternate strips on for color. Slice in half lengthwise, then cut crosswise into thin slices. Place in medium-sized bowl with onion, celery and ginger. Dissolve sugar in vinegar and lemon juice in another bowl. Toss with vegetables and ginger. Refrigerate several hours before serving.

Note: This recipe can be used for different vegetables such as carrot and daikon (giant white radish).

Nutritional Information		*Diabetic Exchanges*	
(per serving)			
Calories	35	Vegetable	1.5
Fat	0 g		
Cholesterol	0 mg		
Sodium	4 mg		

Japanese Pumpkin

2 pounds kabocha (Japanese pumpkin)

1 tablespoon dried shrimp

1 tablespoon vegetable oil

1 tablespoon sugar

1 tablespoon low-sodium shoyu

2 cups water

Cut pumpkin in half; clean out seeds and rinse (leave skin on). Cut into bite-sized pieces and set aside.
Cook remaining ingredients in a large pot over medium heat until sugar dissolves. Add pumpkin and simmer for
10 minutes. Stir once. Continue cooking another 10 minutes or until done (test by piercing with chopstick
or fork).

Nutritional Information		Diabetic Exchanges	
(per serving)			
Calories	70	Bread	1
Fat	2 g		
Cholesterol	6 mg		
Sodium	97 mg		

Oriental Vegetable Dish

$^1/_4$ cup water
2$^1/_2$ cups finely shredded cabbage
1 small onion, chopped
1$^1/_2$ cups bean sprouts
$^1/_2$ cup coarsely shredded carrots
$^1/_2$ cup sliced green bell pepper
$^1/_8$ teaspoon black pepper, or to taste
$^1/_8$ teaspoon Chinese five spice, or to taste

2 teaspoons low-sodium shoyu
$^1/_2$ teaspoon prepared mustard
1 tablespoon sesame oil
$^1/_2$ tablespoon sesame seeds
$^1/_4$ cup water chestnuts

Bring water to a boil in a large saucepan. Add cabbage, onion, beansprouts, carrots and bell pepper; cover and cook for about 5 minutes or until cabbage is crisp-tender, stirring occasionally. Drain. Blend pepper, five spice, shoyu, mustard, sesame oil and sesame seeds in a small bowl. Add to vegetables with water chestnuts and toss lightly to mix. Heat for several minutes and serve.

Nutritional Information		*Diabetic Exchanges*	
(per serving)			
Calories	65	Vegetable	1.5
Fat	3 g	Fat	0.5
Cholesterol	0 mg		
Sodium	61 mg		

Miso Bittermelon

5 bittermelons
1 tablespoon sesame oil
3 tablespoons miso
$^3/_4$ cup sugar
$^1/_2$–1 teaspoon mirin

Cut bittermelons in half lengthwise and remove seeds; slice thin. In a skillet, sauté bittermelon in sesame oil, then add miso, sugar and mirin. Cook until melons shrink to half the original size. Serve hot.

Nutritional Information		Diabetic Exchanges	
(per serving)			
Calories	120	Bread	1.5
Fat	2 g		
Cholesterol	0 mg		
Sodium	239 mg		

Spicy Eggplant

Non-stick cooking spray

5 medium long eggplants (or 1 large round eggplant), sliced diagonally into $1/2$- to 1-inch pieces

$1/4$–$1/2$ teaspoon crushed chili peppers

2 cloves garlic, minced

1 2-inch piece ginger, minced

2–3 stalks green onion, finely chopped

Sauce:

2 tablespoons low-sodium shoyu

$1/2$ cup water

$1/4$ teaspoon black pepper

1 teaspoon sugar (optional)

1 teaspoon vinegar

4 teaspoons cornstarch

1 teaspoon sesame seeds

Combine sauce ingredients in a small bowl; set aside. Coat bottom of a large skillet with non-stick cooking spray. Stir-fry eggplant, chili peppers, garlic and ginger until slightly brown. Cover and steam until eggplant is tender; add green onions. Add sauce to vegetable mixture and cook until thickened, stirring gently. Serve hot.

Nutritional Information

(per serving)

Calories	30
Fat	0 g
Cholesterol	0 mg
Sodium	95 mg

Diabetic Exchanges

Vegetable	1

Broccoli with Oyster Sauce

1 pound broccoli or Chinese broccoli
1/4 cup defatted, reduced-sodium broth (or water)
   Non-stick cooking spray
1 1/2 tablespoons oyster sauce
1/2 teaspoon sesame oil
1/8 teaspoon black pepper

Wash broccoli and cut into 4- to 5-inch pieces. Coat skillet or wok with non-stick cooking spray and stir-fry broccoli for 4 to 5 minutes. Add broth and cook until broccoli is bright green and crisp-tender. Remove broccoli to serving plate, keeping broth in skillet. Add oyster sauce, sesame oil and pepper and stir; simmer for 1 to 2 minutes. Pour over broccoli and serve.

Note: For a thicker sauce, add 1–2 teaspoons cornstarch to broth mixture; cook to desired consistency.

Nutritional Information		Diabetic Exchanges	
(per serving)			
Calories	30	Vegetable	1
Fat	1 g		
Cholesterol	0 mg		
Sodium	311 mg		

Bean Sprout Sanbaizu

2 cups boiling water
1¼ pounds bean sprouts, rinsed
1–2 tablespoons sugar
2 tablespoons vinegar
1 tablespoon shoyu
1–2 tablespoons sesame oil

Boil bean sprouts for 3 to 4 minutes. Drain and cool in ice water, then drain again. To make dressing, mix together sugar, vinegar, shoyu and sesame oil. Pour over bean sprouts and toss. Refrigerate until ready to serve.

Note: Use low-sodium shoyu to lower sodium content.

Nutritional Information		Diabetic Exchanges	
(per serving)			
Calories	80	Bread	1
Fat	2 g		
Cholesterol	0 mg		
Sodium	266 mg		

Watercress and Bean Sprouts
with Sesame Sauce

1½ pounds watercress (about 2 bunches)
1 (12-ounce) package bean sprouts

Sesame sauce:
1 tablespoon sesame seeds
½ cup low-sodium shoyu
2 tablespoons sugar
   Bonito flakes

Blanch watercress in boiling water for 1 minute; drain and cut into 2-inch lengths. Blanch bean sprouts for 1 minute; drain and set aside. Heat sesame seeds in a small, non-stick skillet until golden brown. In a small bowl, mix shoyu, sugar and sesame seeds. Toss vegetables with sauce and top with bonito flakes.

Nutritional Information		Diabetic Exchanges	
(per serving)			
Calories	85	Bread	1
Fat	2 g		
Cholesterol	0 mg		
Sodium	755 mg		

Snow Peas Oriental

Non-stick cooking spray

1 teaspoon sesame oil

2 cloves garlic, crushed

1/2 cup thinly, diagonally sliced carrot

1/2 cup diced onion

1/2 cup sliced water chestnuts

1/2 pound fresh snow (Chinese) peas, trimmed, cut in half OR 2 (6 ounce) packages frozen Chinese peas, thawed

1/2 cup thinly sliced fresh mushrooms

1/2 cup defatted, reduced-sodium chicken broth

2 teaspoons low-sodium shoyu

2 teaspoons cornstarch

Coat a large skillet or wok with non-stick cooking spray. Heat sesame oil and add garlic, carrot, onion and water chestnuts. Sauté for 2–3 minutes or until vegetables are crisp-tender. Add snow peas, mushrooms and broth. Cover and simmer for 3 to 4 minutes or until vegetables are tender. Combine shoyu and cornstarch; stir until cornstarch is dissolved; add to vegetables. Cook over low heat, stirring constantly, until sauce thickens. Serve hot.

Nutritional Information

(per serving)

Calories	50	
Fat	1 g	
Cholesterol	0 mg	
Sodium	107 mg	

Diabetic Exchanges

Vegetable	2

Bara Sushi

⅓ cup sugar

½ cup rice vinegar

¼ teaspoon salt

4 cups hot cooked rice

1 ounce dried shiitake mushrooms (4-5 pieces), soaked, stems removed and caps slivered

1 (6-ounce) can seasoned clams, undrained

½ cup julienned carrots

½ cup julienned green beans

2 aburage, slivered

3 ounces kamaboko (steamed fish cake), slivered

1 (10-ounce) package frozen peas, thawed

1 sheet tamagoyaki,* slivered

1 (1.05-ounce) package furikake nori

¼ cup slivered pickled red ginger

Heat sugar, vinegar and salt in a small pot until sugar dissolves; set aside to cool. Add to hot rice and mix thoroughly. Cook mushrooms, clams, carrots, aburage and green beans in another pot until carrots are crisp-tender, stirring occasionally. Stir vegetable mixture, kamaboko and peas into rice. Top with tamagoyaki, nori and red ginger. Serve hot.

*Beat 1 egg in a small bowl. Coat a small skillet with non-stick cooking spray. Pour egg into a thin sheet and cook, turning once.

Nutritional Information		Diabetic Exchanges	
(per 3/4 cup serving)			
Calories	305	Bread	4
Fat	1 g		
Cholesterol	24 mg		
Sodium	262 mg		

Spicy Peanut Noodles

1 tablespoon sesame oil

½–1 teaspoon dried red pepper flakes

3 tablespoons honey

3 tablespoons low-sodium shoyu

8 ounces uncooked spaghetti, elbow macaroni or other type of noodle

2–3 tablespoons chopped Chinese parsley

2 tablespoons chopped raw blanched peanuts

¼ cup minced green onion

1 teaspoon toasted sesame seeds

Garnish:

Chinese parsley

Heat oil in saucepan; roast red pepper flakes for a few minutes to bring out flavor. Stir in honey and shoyu. Remove from heat and set aside. Cook pasta in boiling, unsalted water until tender. Drain well and combine with sauce. Cover and refrigerate for at least 4 hours or overnight. At serving time, add Chinese parsley, peanuts and green onion to noodles; toss and sprinkle with sesame seeds. Heat in microwave on high for 4 to 5 minutes or until hot. Garnish with Chinese parsley and serve.

Nutritional Information		*Diabetic Exchanges*	
(per serving)			
Calories	135	Bread	1.5
Fat	3 g	Fat	0.5
Cholesterol	0 mg		
Sodium	236 mg		

Barbecue Baked Beans

1 (15 to 16-ounce) can each:
  Baked beans
  Kidney beans
  Black beans
  Lima beans
  Pinto beans
  Cannelini beans
1 large Golden Delicious apple, cored and sliced

1 large onion, coarsely sliced
1 (8-ounce) can no-salt added tomato sauce
³/₄ cup ketchup
1 tablespoon Worcestershire sauce
¹/₄ cup light-brown sugar
¹/₄ teaspoon liquid smoke
¹/₂ teaspoon black pepper, or to taste (optional)

Preheat oven to 325 degrees. Drain and rinse all beans except baked beans. Combine all ingredients and adjust seasonings to taste. Bake uncovered in a 13 x 9-inch pan for 2 hours, stirring every ¹/₂ hour to prevent scorching.

Note: Experiment with different types of beans!

Nutritional Information
(per serving)

Calories	320
Fat	1 g
Cholesterol	0 mg
Sodium	401 mg

Diabetic Exchanges

Bread	4.0
Lean meat	0.5

Oven-Baked French Fries

Non-stick cooking spray
4 medium potatoes
1 tablespoon vegetable oil
¼ teaspoon salt
1 tablespoon malt vinegar

Preheat oven to 475 degrees. Scrub potatoes (do not peel) and slice ½-inch thick. Place oil in a plastic bag and add potato slices; shake well to coat evenly. Place potatoes in a single layer on a baking sheet coated with non-stick cooking spray. Bake for 25 to 30 minutes, turning every 10 minutes. Sprinkle with salt, if desired, and serve with malt vinegar.

Nutritional Information   Diabetic Exchanges

(per serving)				
Calories	180		Bread	2.0
Fat	3 g		Fat	0.5
Cholesterol	0 mg			
Sodium	145 mg			

Char Siu Bao

Dough:
3½ cups all-purpose flour, divided
1 tablespoon shortening
¼ cup sugar, divided
1 package active dry yeast
1 cup warm water, divided

Filling:
½ pound char siu (fat removed), diced
4 tablespoons chopped green onion
2½ tablespoons sugar
4 teaspoons low-sodium shoyu
½ teaspoon sesame oil
2 teaspoons flour
2 teaspoons cornstarch
¼ cup water

Dough: Put 3 cups flour in a large bowl; cut in shortening and stir in 2 tablespoons sugar. In a small bowl, mix 2 tablespoons sugar, yeast and ⅓ cup warm water, stirring until yeast dissolves. Add remaining ½ cup flour and mix well. Combine flour and yeast mixtures and remaining ⅔ cup water. Knead on a lightly floured surface for 5 minutes or until dough is smooth and elastic. Place in a greased bowl; cover with a damp cloth and let rise until doubled. Punch down and divide into 18 portions. Flatten each portion and put about 1 tablespoon filling in the center, pull dough up and around filling; pinch to seal. Place seam-side down on squares of waxed paper; let rest 20 to 30 minutes. Steam over boiling water on rack or in steamer for 15 minutes or until dough is cooked.

Filling: Heat oil in a saucepan and stir-fry char siu for 30 seconds. Add green onion, sugar and shoyu. Mix flour and cornstarch with water; stir into char siu. Cook until mixture thickens; cool.

Nutritional Information		Diabetic Exchanges	
(per 1 bun serving)			
Calories	135	Bread	1.5
Fat	2 g	Lean meat	0.5
Cholesterol	8 mg		
Sodium	83 mg		

Nā iʻa

Main Dishes

Laulau

Original

1 pound salted butterfish
2 pounds pork butt
48 luau leaves
12 ti leaves

Reduced

1 pound unsalted butterfish
1 pound unsalted salmon
2 pounds taro, cut in ½-inch cubes
1 onion, sliced
3 cloves garlic, minced
2 teaspoons ginger, minced
½ teaspoon Hawaiian salt
48 luau leaves
12 ti leaves

Cut fish into six pieces and divide taro into six portions. Wash luau leaves and remove outer skin of stem. Wash ti leaves. Combine fish with onion, garlic, ginger and salt. Lay two ti leaves on table and place 8 luau leaves in center. Place one portion each of taro and fish on luau leaves, folding leaves over fish to form a bundle. Tie end of ti leaves. Steam for 4 hours.

Nutritional Information (per serving)				Diabetic Exchanges			
Original		Reduced		Original		Reduced	
Calories	605	Calories	445	Vegetable	1	Vegetable	1.0
Fat	37 g	Fat	10 g	Medium-fat meat	7	Bread	1.5
Cholesterol	182 mg	Cholesterol	83 mg	Fat	0.5	Lean meat	5.0
Sodium	992 mg	Sodium	311mg				

Chicken Luau

Original

2½ pounds chicken thighs
1½ teaspoons salt
1½ cups coconut milk
  2 pounds luau leaves

Reduced

2 pounds skinless chicken thighs
1 clove garlic, minced
6 cups defatted chicken broth
2 pounds fresh or 2 cups cooked ready-to-serve
   luau leaves
1½ cups non-fat dry milk powder
½ teaspoon salt
½ teaspoon coconut extract

Sauté chicken and garlic in a large skillet. Add 2 cups broth and simmer. In a large pot, cook fresh luau leaves in 2 cups broth for 20 to 30 minutes. Make a paste with 1 cup broth, milk powder, salt and coconut extract. Combine paste with chicken and luau leaves; heat through.

Nutritional Information (per serving)

Original		Reduced	
Calories	375	Calories	285
Fat	27 g	Fat	12 g
Cholesterol	102 mg	Cholesterol	100 mg
Sodium	692 mg	Sodium	523mg

Diabetic Exchanges

Original		Reduced	
Vegetable	1	Vegetable	1.0
Lean meat	4	Lean meat	3.0
Fat	3	Fat	1.0
		Skim milk	0.5

Chili

Original

- 1 pound ground beef
- $1/2$ cup each chopped onion and celery
- 1 clove garlic, minced
- $1/2$ package chili seasoning
- $1/4$ teaspoon black pepper
- $1/2$ teaspoon cumin
- $3/4$ teaspoon chili powder
- $1/4$ teaspoon garlic salt
- $1/4$ teaspoon salt
- 2 (8-ounce) cans tomato sauce
- 1 cup each canned pinto and kidney beans, drained

Reduced

- 1 pound lean ground turkey
- $1/2$ cup chopped onion
- $1/4$ cup each chopped green bell pepper and celery
- 1 clove garlic, minced
- $1/2$ teaspoon oregano
- $1/4$ teaspoon black pepper
- 1 teaspoon cumin
- 1 tablespoon chili powder
- 2 (8-ounce) cans no-salt-added tomato sauce
- 1 teaspoon brown sugar
- 1 cup each canned pinto and kidney beans, drained

Starting with a cold pan, sauté ground turkey, onion, green bell pepper, celery, garlic, oregano, black pepper, cumin and chili powder. Add tomato sauce, sugar and beans; simmer at least 30 minutes.

Nutritional Information (per serving)				Diabetic Exchanges			
Original		Reduced		Original		Reduced	
Calories	285	Calories	190	Vegetable	1	Vegetable	1
Fat	16.5 g	Fat	8 g	Bread	1	Bread	1
Cholesterol	68 mg	Cholesterol	38 mg	Medium-fat meat	2	Lean meat	2
Sodium	1050 mg	Sodium	420 mg	Fat	1		

Shrimp Curry

Original

- ¹/₂ cup butter
- 2 medium onions, chopped
- 2 apples, pared and diced
- 1¹/₂ tablespoons curry powder
- 1¹/₂ tablespoons light-brown sugar
- 2 cloves garlic, minced
- 1 teaspoon minced ginger
- 2 cups chicken broth
- 6 tablespoons flour
- 1 (12-ounce) can frozen coconut milk, thawed
- 1¹/₂ teaspoons salt
- 2 cups cooked shrimp

Reduced

- 1 tablespoon canola oil
- 2 medium onions, chopped
- 2 apples, pared and diced
- 1¹/₂ tablespoons curry powder
- 1¹/₂ tablespoons light-brown sugar
- 2 cloves garlic, minced
- 1 teaspoon minced ginger
- 2³/₄ cups defatted chicken broth
- 6 tablespoons flour
- 1 cup non-fat milk powder
- ¹/₂ cup coconut milk
- ¹/₂ teaspoon coconut extract
- ¹/₂ teaspoon salt
- 2 cups cooked shrimp

Heat oil in skillet and sauté onion and apple until clear. Stir in curry powder, sugar, garlic and ginger; cook 10 to 15 minutes. Add 1 cup chicken broth and simmer for 45 to 50 minutes. Combine next five ingredients with remaining chicken broth; add to skillet and cook until thick. (Do not boil or sauce will curdle.) Stir in shrimp and heat through.

Nutritional Information (per serving)

Original		Reduced	
Calories	455	Calories	295
Fat	29 g	Fat	8 g
Cholesterol	245 mg	Cholesterol	205 mg
Sodium	1,164 mg	Sodium	804 mg

Diabetic Exchanges

Original		Reduced	
Lean meat	2	Lean meat	2.0
Fat	6	Fat	1.0
Fruit	1	Low-fat milk	0.5
		Fruit	1.0

Egg Foo Yung

Original

6 eggs

1 cup bean sprouts

1 cup fresh or drained canned shrimp

1/4 cup sliced or chopped water chestnuts

1/2 cup finely sliced onion

1/2 teaspoon salt

   Dash of black pepper

1/2 cup oil

Gravy:

1 cup chicken broth

1 tablespoon shoyu

1/2 teaspoon sugar

   Scant tablespoon cornstarch

Reduced

2 eggs

8 egg whites

1 cup bean sprouts

1 cup fresh shrimp, chopped, or diced cooked chicken breast

1/4 cup sliced or chopped water chestnuts

1/2 cup finely sliced onion

1/4 teaspoon black pepper

   Non-stick cooking spray

Gravy:

1 cup defatted chicken broth

1 tablespoon low-sodium shoyu

1/2 teaspoon sugar

   Scant tablespoon cornstarch

Egg Foo Yung
(continued)

Beat eggs and egg whites lightly. Add bean sprouts, shrimp or chicken, water chestnuts, onion and pepper. Mix gently but thoroughly. Lightly coat a non-stick skillet with cooking spray and heat over medium-high heat. Drop about 1/2 cup egg mixture into pan for each patty. Brown on both sides, cooking until bean sprouts are tender but still crisp. Combine gravy ingredients in a small bowl and add to pan; cook until smooth and thickened. Pour over patties and serve.

Note: Replace bean sprouts, onions and water chestnuts with one package chop suey vegetables. To reduce sodium, use low-sodium or sodium-free defatted chicken broth.

Nutritional Information (per serving)

Original		Reduced	
Calories	325	Calories	160
Fat	22 g	Fat	4 g
Cholesterol	420 mg	Cholesterol	212 mg
Sodium	945 mg	Sodium	570 mg

Diabetic Exchanges

Original		Reduced	
Medium-fat meat	2	Lean meat	2
Fat	4		

Baked Opakapaka
with Soy Ginger Sauce

4 (5-ounce) opakapaka fillets

3 stalks green onion, julienned (reserve some for garnish)

1 2-inch piece ginger, sliced

$^1/_2$ cup defatted chicken broth

2 tablespoons low-sodium shoyu

2 tablespoons rice vinegar

$^1/_4$ cup sake

1 teaspoon sugar

Dash of liquid hot pepper sauce

1 teaspoon cornstarch mixed with 2 tablespoons water

Mix all ingredients except opakapaka and reserved green onion. Place opakapaka in a small, shallow baking pan and pour sauce over. Bake covered at 425 degrees for about 15 minutes. Remove from oven and place on a serving platter and keep warm. Pour pan juices into a small pot and boil for 1 minute. Add cornstarch mixed with water and cook and stir until thickened. Pour over opakapaka and garnish with green onion.

Nutritional Information   Diabetic Exchanges

(per serving)

Calories	180	Lean meat 3.5
Fat	2 g	
Cholesterol	56 mg	
Sodium	431 mg	

Simmered Onaga with Somen

Serves 6

2 cups water
½ cup low-sodium shoyu
⅓ cup regular shoyu
2½ tablespoons sake
⅓ cup sugar
1 tablespoon shredded bonito flakes
3 tablespoons chopped green onion
2 teaspoons minced ginger

1 clove garlic, minced
2 teaspoons rice vinegar
2½ pounds red or pink snapper fillets
1 tablespoon cornstarch (mix with a little water)
5 cups cooked somen

In a skillet, combine first 10 ingredients and bring to a boil. Reduce heat to low and add fish fillets. Cover skillet and simmer for 15 minutes or until fish is done; remove fish. Add cornstarch paste to skillet, cooking and stirring until sauce thickens. Place fish over somen and top with sauce.

Note: To reduce sodium level use only low-sodium shoyu and decrease the total amount in the recipe.

Nutritional Information

(per serving)

Calories	475
Fat	3 g
Cholesterol	78 mg
Sodium	2,080 mg

Diabetic Exchanges

Bread	2.5
Lean meat	6.0

Baked Ono

Serves
6

6 (5-ounce) portions ono fillets
2 tablespoons lime juice
1/2 teaspoon minced garlic
2 teaspoons minced shallot
1/2 tablespoon chopped fresh rosemary
1/2 tablespoon chopped fresh thyme
1/2 cup sliced fresh shiitake mushrooms
1 1/2 teaspoons julienned ginger

Dash of white pepper
1/8 cup chopped Chinese parsley
1 small carrot, julienned
1/3 cup water
3 tablespoons chopped green onion (optional)

Place ono fillets in a baking dish. Combine lime juice, garlic, shallot, herbs, mushroom, ginger, pepper, Chinese parsley and carrot; pour over fillets. Add water and cover with foil. Bake in a 350-degree oven for 15 to 20 minutes. Garnish with chopped green onion, if desired.

Nutritional Information		Diabetic Exchanges	
(per serving)			
Calories	195	Lean meat	4
Fat	6 g		
Cholesterol	58 mg		
Sodium	137 mg		

Fish with Sesame

2 pounds fish steaks or fillets

1/4 cup orange juice

2 tablespoons ketchup

1 tablespoon low-sodium shoyu

1 tablespoon lemon juice

1/4 teaspoon white pepper

3/4 teaspoon sesame oil

1 tablespoon sugar

1 1/2 teaspoons cornstarch

1 tablespoon sesame seeds, toasted

Heat orange juice, ketchup, shoyu, lemon juice, pepper, sesame oil, sugar and cornstarch in a small saucepan over medium heat. Cook fish over barbecue grill or broil in oven; place on serving platter and pour sauce over. Sprinkle with toasted sesame seeds.

Nutritional Information

(per serving)

Calories	350
Fat	9 g
Cholesterol	93 mg
Sodium	325 mg

Diabetic Exchanges

Fruit	1
Lean meat	5

Fish with Tomato Sauce

1¹/₂ pounds ahi fillets, cut into 1-inch cubes

1¹/₂ tablespoons olive oil

¹/₂ cup coarsely chopped onion

¹/₂ cup coarsley chopped green bell pepper

2 cloves garlic, minced

1 (1 pound, 12-ounce) can whole tomatoes, drained and coarsely chopped

¹/₂ cup dry white wine

¹/₂ teaspoon fresh thyme (or ¹/₄ teaspoon dried)

¹/₂ teaspoon dried oregano

¹/₈ teaspoon black pepper

1 bay leaf

1 teaspoon minced parsley

Heat olive oil in a large skillet and sauté onion, green bell pepper and garlic until tender, about 2 to 3 minutes. Add tomatoes, white wine, thyme, oregano, black pepper and bay leaf. Blend well. Bring sauce to a boil, reduce heat and simmer uncovered for 15 minutes or until slightly thickened. Place fish on top of tomato sauce. Simmer covered for 10 to 15 minutes, or until fish flakes easily when tested with a fork. Sprinkle with minced parsley. Serve immediately.

Nutritional Information		Diabetic Exchanges	
(per serving)			
Calories	280	Vegetable	2.0
Fat	8 g	Lean meat	3.5
Cholesterol	62 mg	Fat	1.0
Sodium	337 mg		

Broiled Swordfish

Serves
6

2 pounds swordfish or marlin

2 tablespoons reduced-calorie mayonnaise

2 cloves garlic, minced

    Ground black pepper to taste

2 tablespoons panko flakes (flour meal for breading)

    Juice and grated rind of 1 lemon

1 teaspoon honey

    Parsley or mint leaves, finely chopped

Combine mayonnaise and garlic; spread on fillets. Sprinkle with pepper and panko flakes. Combine lemon juice, rind and honey; drizzle on top of fillets. Grill over hot coals for 5 to 8 minutes each side, or until fish is opaque throughout. Garnish with parsley or mint.

Nutritional Information

(per serving)

Calories	260
Fat	9 g
Cholesterol	77 mg
Sodium	215 mg

Diabetic Exchanges

Lean meat	4

Nori Salmon

4 salmon fillets (1$^1/_2$ inches thick, about
  5 ounces each)
8 pieces yaki nori

Soy Wasabi Vinaigrette:
$^1/_4$ cup sugar
$^1/_4$ cup shoyu
 3 tablespoons rice vinegar
 1 tablespoon lime juice
$^1/_8$ teaspoon white pepper
 2 stalks green onion
   wasabi to taste

In a small pot, heat ingredients for vinaigrette. Keep warm. Salt and pepper salmon fillets to taste. Wrap salmon with nori using two pieces per fillet. Heat non-stick skillet and sear salmon on both sides until desired doneness. Serve with vinaigrette.

Nutritional Information		Diabetic Exchanges	
(per serving)			
Calories	220	Lean meat	4
Fat	8 g		
Cholesterol	55 mg		
Sodium	550 mg		

Salmon Hot Pot

4 cups water

1/2 small onion, finely chopped

3 cloves garlic, minced

3 tablespoons crushed ginger

1/3 cup sake

1 tablespoon mirin

1 tablespoon shoyu

1/2 teaspoon Hawaiian salt

1 medium potato, diced

2 carrots, diagonally sliced

1 pound salmon, skinned, cut into bite-sized chunks

1/2 block firm tofu

3 stalks green onion

5–6 leaves won bok cabbage, thinly sliced

5 ounces fresh mushrooms, sliced

Boil water, onion, garlic, ginger, sake, mirin, shoyu and Hawaiian salt for 5 to 10 minutes. Add potato and carrots; cook until tender yet still firm. Add salmon and cook until almost done. Stir in tofu, green onion, won bok and mushrooms. Serve.

Nutritional Information

(per serving)

Calories	230
Fat	8 g
Cholesterol	50 mg
Sodium	498 mg

Diabetic Exchanges

Vegetable	1.0
Lean meat	3.0
Bread	0.5

String Beans, Carrots and Shrimp

1½ pounds fresh string beans

¼ pound lean pork

1½ tablespoons vegetable oil

2 large garlic cloves, peeled and crushed

½ teaspoon sugar

1 teaspoon fish sauce

3 carrots, thinly sliced

½ pound medium shrimp

Dash of black pepper

Chinese parsley for garnish

Remove ends of string beans and cut in half diagonally. Trim any visible fat from pork and slice thin. Heat oil in skillet with garlic. Stir-fry pork, sugar and fish sauce for about 2 minutes. Add string beans, carrots and ½ cup water; cover and steam 10 minutes. Stir in shrimp and cook 5 minutes. (If using cooked shrimp, just heat through.) Mix well and transfer to a serving plate. Garnish with pepper and chopped Chinese parsley.

Nutritional Information

(per serving)

Calories	140
Fat	5 g
Cholesterol	67 mg
Sodium	216 mg

Diabetic Exchanges

Vegetable	2.5
Lean meat	1.0
Fat	0.5

Shrimp with Black Beans

1 tablespoon vegetable oil

4 ounces lean ground turkey

3 tablespoons fermented salted black beans, rinsed
and drained

1 green bell pepper, seeded and finely chopped

12 ounces fresh mushrooms, thinly sliced

3 cloves garlic, minced

1 tablespoon minced ginger

12 ounces shrimp, cleaned and deveined

1 cup defatted, reduced-sodium chicken broth

2 tablespoons oyster sauce

1 tablespoon cornstarch

Chopped green onion for garnish

Heat oil in a large non-stick skillet and stir-fry turkey, black beans, green bell pepper, mushrooms, garlic and ginger for about 3 minutes. Add shrimp and cook for 3 more minutes. Combine broth, oyster sauce and cornstarch; add to skillet and bring to a boil, stirring until thickened. Place in serving dish and sprinkle with green onion.

Nutritional Information		*Diabetic Exchanges*	
(per serving)			
Calories	180	Lean meat	2.5
Fat	6 g	Fat	1.0
Cholesterol	107 mg		
Sodium	450 mg		

Fried Shrimp

2 pounds raw shrimp

2 cloves garlic, minced

1 tablespoon minced ginger

1 tablespoon chopped Chinese parsley

1 tablespoon sesame oil

1 tablespoon dry white wine

1½ tablespoons low-sodium shoyu

   Chopped green onion for garnish

Combine all ingredients, except for the garnish, and marinate for 30 minutes. Stir-fry shrimp with marinade in a non-stick skillet until shrimp are done but not overcooked. Place in serving dish, sprinkle with chopped green onion and serve.

Nutritional Information		Diabetic Exchanges	
(per serving)			
Calories	190	Lean meat	3.0
Fat	5 g	Fat	0.5
Cholesterol	310 mg		
Sodium	440 mg		

Linguine with Clam Sauce

8 ounces linguine, cooked according to package
  directions

2 (6½ ounce) cans chopped clams, drained, juice
  reserved

3 cloves garlic, minced

¼ cup chopped parsley

1 teaspoon Worcestershire sauce

¾ cup non-fat sour cream

¼ cup non-fat cream cheese

¼ cup skim milk

¼ cup chopped roasted red bell pepper or pimentos,
  drained and chopped

⅛ teaspoon white pepper

Lightly coat a non-stick pan with non-stick cooking spray. Sauté garlic lightly (do not brown). Add clams,
3 tablespoons reserved clam juice, parsley and Worcestershire sauce; simmer for 2 minutes. Reduce heat and add
sour cream, cream cheese and skim milk, stirring constantly until heated through. Stir in red bell pepper and
white pepper. Serve over pasta and garnish with parsley.

Note: To roast red bell pepper, cut in half and place on baking pan or rack, cut side down close to heating
element. Broil until skins are charred, cool, then rub off charred skin.

Nutritional Information		Diabetic Exchanges	
(per serving)			
Calories	295	Bread	2.0
Fat	2 g	Skim milk	0.5
Cholesterol	40 mg	Lean meat	2.0
Sodium	200 mg		

Red Clam Sauce
with Angel Hair Pasta

1 clove garlic, minced

1 tablespoon olive oil

$^1/_4$ cup dry white wine

1 (16-ounce) can tomatoes

2 tablespoons tomato paste

1 teaspoon dried basil

$^1/_2$ teaspoon dried oregano

2 tablespoons chopped fresh parsley

$^1/_4$ teaspoon black pepper

Juice from $^1/_2$ lemon

1 dozen little neck clams or 2 (10-ounce) cans clams, whole or chopped

8 ounces angel hair pasta, cooked according to package directions

In a large skillet, sauté garlic in oil over medium heat for 2 or 3 minutes. (Do not brown.) Add remaining ingredients except clams and linguine; simmer over low heat for 20 to 25 minutes, stirring and breaking up tomatoes. Stir in whole clams in shells or canned (with juice). Cover and steam whole clams for 10 minutes or until clams open; steam for 3 or 4 minutes if using canned clams. Serve with cooked pasta.

Nutritional Information		Diabetic Exchanges	
(per serving)			
Calories	375	Vegetable	1
Fat	6 g	Bread	2
Cholesterol	50 mg	Lean meat	3
Sodium	420 mg		

Oriental Chicken and Vegetables

1¹/₂ cups chopped skinless chicken breast
  2 medium carrots, sliced
  1 (8-ounce) can water chestnuts, drained
  1 (4-ounce) can button mushroms, drained
¹/₂ cup chopped green onion
  2 stalks celery, sliced

Sauce:
1¹/₂ tablespoons sugar
  4 tablespoons low-sodium shoyu
1¹/₂ tablespoons minced garlic
¹/₂ tablespoon minced ginger
  1 tablespoon sesame oil
¹/₃ cup water
  1 tablespoon sesame seeds (toasted and ground)
    for garnish

Place chicken and vegetables in a pot in the order of ingredients listed. Mix sauce ingredients and add to chicken and vegetables. Bring to a boil and cook approximately 5 minutes. Do not stir or mix. Reduce heat and simmer approximately 20 minutes or until done. Toss gently and serve garnished with sesame seeds.

Nutritional Information

(per serving)

Calories	185
Fat	7 g
Cholesterol	38 mg
Sodium	420 mg

Diabetic Exchanges

Vegetable	2.0
Lean meat	2.0
Fat	0.5

Vegetable-Chicken Stir-fry

4 chicken breast halves, skin and bones removed

$1/4$ cup bottled Oriental barbeque sauce

1 teaspoon sugar

2 cloves garlic, minced

1 teaspoon grated ginger

1 tablespoon macadamia nut oil or peanut oil

1 onion, cut into chunks

1 zucchini, sliced thin

1 long eggplant, sliced thin

1 green bell pepper, cut into $1/2$-inch strips

2 tomatoes, cut into chunks

1 tablespoon cornstarch

2 tablespoons water

3 tablespoons oyster sauce

Rinse chicken breasts and cut into thin strips. In a small bowl, combine barbeque sauce, sugar, garlic and ginger. Add chicken strips and marinate at least 30 minutes. Heat wok with oil; add chicken and stir-fry until brown, then remove from wok. Add onion, zucchini, eggplant and bell pepper with a little bit of water (to deglaze pan and for some moisture); stir-fry for a few minutes. Add tomatoes and chicken, toss, then cover for 5 to 10 minutes to soften vegetables. Mix cornstarch, water and oyster sauce; add to wok, cook and stir until thickened. Serve hot.

Nutritional Information		Diabetic Exchanges	
(per serving)			
Calories	205	Vegetable	1.5
Fat	8 g	Bread	0.5
Cholesterol	44 mg	Lean meat	2.0
Sodium	576 mg	Fat	0.5

Chicken with Ginger

1 tablespoon vegetable oil
1 clove garlic, minced
1 onion, chopped
1 pound boneless, skinless chicken, shredded
1 2-inch piece ginger, minced

Seasoning mixture:
1 tablespoon fish sauce
$1/2$ tablespoon sugar
Pepper to taste
Chinese parsley for garnish

Sauté oil, garlic and onion in a skillet over high heat until light brown. Add shredded chicken, ginger, seasoning mixture and 1 cup cold water. Cover and simmer 20 minutes. Sprinkle with black pepper and garnish with chopped Chinese parsley. Serve hot.

Nutritional Information		Diabetic Exchanges	
(per serving)			
Calories	175	Lean meat	2.5
Fat	8 g	Fat	1.0
Cholesterol	63 mg		
Sodium	368 mg		

Herbert's Hawaiian Stew

1 pound taro, peeled and cut into 1-inch cubes

1 pound breadfruit, peeled and cut into 1-inch cubes

1 onion, chopped

2 stalks celery, chopped

3 medium carrots, diced

3 tablespoons curry powder

1 slice ginger

4 chicken thighs, skin and bones removed, cubed (reserve bones for stock)

1 bay leaf

1 clove garlic, crushed

$^3/_4$ teaspoon Hawaiian salt

Place all ingredients in a large pot with enough water to cover, adding chicken bones for additional flavor. Bring to a boil, then simmer for 45 minutes or until taro is tender. Simmer longer for a thicker stew or add 2 tablespoons flour mixed with $^1/_4$ cup water. Remove bones before serving.

Note: To prevent an allergic reaction when handling raw taro, wear gloves or rub your hands well with cooking oil. No part of the taro plant should be eaten raw because it contains calcium oxalate crystals (calcified nutrients), which break down during cooking.

Nutritional Information
(per serving)

Calories	330
Fat	5 g
Cholesterol	51 mg
Sodium	350 mg

Diabetic Exchanges

Vegetable	1.0
Bread	2.5
Lean meat	2.0

Sweet Barbecue Chicken

2 pounds boneless, skinless chicken, visible fat
  removed

2 tablespoons vegetable oil

2 cloves garlic, minced

$^1/_2$ cup guava jelly

2 tablespoons fresh lemon juice

1 tablespoon light-brown sugar

$^1/_2$ teaspoon salt

1 tablespoon shoyu

$^1/_2$ teaspoon allspice

1 tablespoon cornstarch

3 tablespoons water

Heat oil in a large skillet and brown chicken. Add garlic and $^1/_3$ cup water; simmer for 10 minutes. In a small saucepan, combine jelly, lemon juice, sugar, salt, shoyu and allspice; bring to a boil. Combine cornstarch and water; add to saucepan and cook and stir until sauce thickens. Pour over chicken in skillet; cover and simmer 15 minutes. Remove cover and continue cooking until sauce reduces to the consistency of syrup.

Nutritional Information

(per serving)

Calories	240
Fat	9 g
Cholesterol	72 mg
Sodium	304 mg

Diabetic Exchanges

Lean meat	3.0
Fat	0.5
Fruit	1.0

Plum Chicken

¹/₂ cup plum jam

¹/₂ teaspoon sesame oil

2 tablespoons balsamic vinegar

1 tablespoon lime juice

2 tablespoons grated ginger

3 tablespoons dry sherry

¹/₂ cup defatted chicken broth

¹/₂ teaspoon salt

4 boneless, skinless chicken breast halves, visible fat removed

Combine first seven ingredients and set aside. Sprinkle chicken with ¹/₂ teaspoon salt and pepper to taste; sear in a heated non-stick skillet until golden brown on both sides. Place in a small, shallow baking pan and pour sauce over. Bake at 350 degrees for 30 minutes, basting frequently. Remove from oven and place on a serving platter and keep warm. Transfer remaining sauce into a small pot; cook until reduced by half. Pour over chicken and garnish with Chinese parsley.

Nutritional Information

(per serving)

Calories	320
Fat	7 g
Cholesterol	82 mg
Sodium	423 mg

Diabetic Exchanges

Lean meat	4
Fruit	2

Mango Chutney Chicken

2¼ cups long grain white rice (3 rice cooker measuring cups)

3 cups defatted chicken broth

½ cup raisins

1 banana, cut into chunks

½ teaspoon thyme

⅛ teaspoon white pepper

Sauce:

½ cup mango chutney

2 tablespoons Dijon mustard

2 teaspoons curry powder

1 teaspoon thyme

⅛ teaspoon white pepper

2 tablespoons lime juice

½ cup white wine

4 chicken breast halves, skin, bones and visible fat removed

Wash rice. Mix all ingredients and cook in a rice cooker or simmer until done. Combine all sauce ingredients except chicken. Score chicken breast (to absorb the sauce) and place in a small, shallow baking pan; pour sauce over. Bake for 35 to 40 minutes at 375 degrees. Remove chicken from oven and keep warm. Pour sauce into a small pan and simmer until reduced by half. Spoon rice mixture onto a serving platter and arrange chicken on top. Pour sauce over chicken and garnish with parsley.

Note: Use reduced sodium broth to reduce sodium content.

Nutritional Information		Diabetic Exchanges	
(per serving)			
Calories	760	Fruit	3
Fat	8 g	Bread	4
Cholesterol	82 mg	Lean meat	4
Sodium	773 mg		

Ono Zesty Chicken

4 chicken breast halves, skin, bones and
  visible fat removed

1 teaspoon poultry seasoning

1 teaspoon liquid hot pepper sauce

$^1/_2$ tablespoon dried oregano

1 teaspoon dried basil

$1^1/_2$ teaspoons garlic powder

$^1/_2$ teaspoon sage

1 teaspoon minced ginger

$^1/_8$ cup fresh lime juice

Rinse chicken in cold water and shake off excess. Combine remaining ingredients and coat chicken with mixture. Marinate in refrigerator for at least 2 hours. Wrap chicken in foil and bake in a 350-degree oven for 30 minutes.

Nutritional Information

(per serving)

		Diabetic Exchanges	
Calories	185	Lean meat	3.5
Fat	7 g		
Cholesterol	82 mg		
Sodium	76 mg		

Chicken Long Rice

2 (1¾-ounce) bundles long rice

1 tablespoon oil

2½ pounds boneless, skinless chicken breasts, cubed

2–4 cloves garlic, minced

6 cups defatted chicken broth

1 tablespoon slivered ginger

1 teaspoon salt

1 (6-ounce) can whole mushrooms, drained

3 tablespoons thinly sliced green onion

Soak long rice in warm water for 30 minutes; cut into 2-inch lengths. Heat oil in a large skillet and sauté chicken and garlic just until browned. Add broth, ginger and salt; bring to a boil then simmer 1 hour or until chicken is tender. Stir in long rice and mushrooms; simmer 10 minutes. Sprinkle with green onion just before serving.

Note: To reduce sodium content, use low-sodium chicken broth and omit salt. Substitute Chinese black mushrooms for canned whole mushrooms. (If dried, soak in warm water for 15 minutes, remove stem and slice.)

Nutritional Information		Diabetic Exchanges	
(per serving)			
Calories	220	Bread	1.0
Fat	6 g	Lean meat	2.5
Cholesterol	73 mg		
Sodium	675 mg		

Asparagus Chicken

2 pounds fresh asparagus

12 ounces boneless, skinless chicken breast

2 tablespoons vegetable oil

1 cup chopped onion

8 ounces fresh mushrooms, sliced

3 tablespoons oyster sauce

Parboil asparagus and cut into 1-inch lengths. Remove visible fat from chicken, cut into bite-sized pieces and brown in hot oil. Stir-fry onion for 2 to 3 minutes, then stir-fry mushrooms and asparagus for 2 to 3 minutes. Add oyster sauce and mix well.

Nutritional Information		*Diabetic Exchanges*	
(per serving)			
Calories	155	Vegetable	2
Fat	6 g	Lean meat	1
Cholesterol	36 mg	Fat	1
Sodium	242 mg		

Pancit

4 ounces chicken breast, skin and bones removed

3 ounces shrimp, shelled and sliced

8 ounces lean pork, sliced

1 teaspoon minced garlic

2 tablespoons chopped onion

2 cups shredded cabbage

1 cup sliced carrots

8 ounces fine, thin noodles (miki)

1 tablespoon shoyu

2 tablespoons peanut oil, divided

Chicken broth (unsalted)

Sauté chicken, shrimp, pork, garlic and onion in 2 teaspoons of the oil and set aside. Do the same with the vegetables. Set aside a portion of each for garnishing. Blanch noodles in boiling chicken broth for about 2 minutes, then stir-fry in 2 teaspoons of the oil. Add vegetables, meat mixture and shoyu. Arrange on platter and garnish with reserved meat and vegetables.

Nutritional Information

(per serving)

Calories	250
Fat	7 g
Cholesterol	44 mg
Sodium	338 mg

Diabetic Exchanges

Vegetable	0.5
Bread	1.5
Lean meat	1.5
Fat	1.0

Chicken Tinola

3–4 cups defatted chicken broth (or water)

1 piece ginger, crushed

1 clove garlic, crushed

½ onion, minced

2 pounds chicken, skin and bones removed,
cut into serving pieces

2 green papayas (or green squashes), peeled and
cut into chunks

2 cups marungay leaves or watercress

Place chicken broth or water, ginger, garlic, onion and chicken in a large pot. Bring to a boil and simmer for 15 to 20 minutes. Add green papaya and marungay leaves; cook just until tender. Serve in a bowl with rice.

Nutritional Information

(per serving)

Calories	225
Fat	7 g
Cholesterol	80 mg
Sodium	266 mg

Diabetic Exchanges

Vegetable	1.0
Fruit	0.5
Lean meat	3.0

Turkey Adobo

2 pounds turkey breast (cut into 2-inch pieces)
1 bay leaf
$^1/_2$ teaspoon peppercorn, crushed
8 cloves garlic, peeled and crushed
$^1/_3$ cup red wine vinegar
1$^2/_3$ tablespoons shoyu

Mix all ingredients and marinate at least 1 hour. Place in heavy-gauged pot. Boil covered for several minutes then reduce heat to low. Cook until turkey is tender, stirring occasionally to prevent scorching. Uncover pot and raise heat to medium. Continue cooking until liquid is reduced and slightly thickened.

Nutritional Information

(per serving)

Calories	130
Fat	5 g
Cholesterol	56 mg
Sodium	265 mg

Diabetic Exchanges

Lean meat	2.5

Tofu and Vegetable Stir-fry

$^1/_2$ cup water

$^1/_4$ cup dry sherry

1 tablespoon cornstarch

1 tablespoon oyster sauce

2 tablespoons low-sodium shoyu

1 packet reduced-sodium chicken bouillon granules

1 teaspoon minced ginger

1 cup thinly sliced carrots

2 cloves garlic, minced

3 cups cut-up broccoli

6 ounces tofu, cubed

1 tablespoon sesame seeds, toasted (optional)

For sauce, stir together water, dry sherry, cornstarch, shoyu, oyster sauce, bouillon granules and ginger. Set aside. Coat a wok or large skillet with non-stick cooking spray and heat over medium-high heat. Stir-fry carrots and garlic for 2 minutes; add broccoli and stir-fry for 3 to 4 minutes or until all vegetables are crisp-tender. Push vegetables from center of wok and add sauce to center, cooking and stirring until thickened and bubbly. Add tofu and cook for 1 minute, stirring to coat tofu and vegetables with sauce. Sprinkle with sesame seeds and serve.

Nutritional Information

(per serving)

Calories	275
Fat	9 g
Cholesterol	0 mg
Sodium	546 mg

Diabetic Exchanges

Vegetable	4.0
Medium-fat meat	2.0
Fat	0.5

Tofu with Tomatoes

2 blocks firm tofu
$^1/_2$ teaspoon salt
1 teaspoon black pepper
1 onion, thinly sliced
3 shallots, minced
1 tablespoon tomato paste
1–2 cloves garlic, minced
$^1/_2$ cup dry white wine

$^1/_2$ cup water
2 packets low-sodium chicken
   bouillon granules
1 bay leaf
3 ripe tomatoes, peeled, seeded and diced
   All-purpose flour
   Minced parsley

Sprinkle tofu with salt and pepper; let stand then drain in colander. Sauté onion and shallots until golden brown in a non- stick pan coated with non-stick cooking spray. Stir in garlic and tomato paste and cook for several more minutes. Add wine and bring to a boil, then add water, bouillon granules, bay leaf and tomatoes. Cut tofu into $^1/_2$-inch slices and dust with flour. In another non-stick pan coated with non-stick cooking spray, sauté tofu until golden brown. Gently place tofu in tomato sauce and simmer over low heat until sauce thickens. Season to taste and garnish with minced parsley.

Nutritional Information

(per serving)

Calories	170
Fat	7 g
Cholesterol	0 mg
Sodium	230 mg

Diabetic Exchanges

Vegetable	1
Medium-fat meat	2

Tuna Tofu Patties

1 can water-packed tuna
1 (20-ounce) block firm tofu, mashed and drained well
2 egg whites
¼ cup grated carrot
¼ cup chopped green onion
1 teaspoon grated ginger (optional)
½ teaspoon salt
   Pepper to taste
2–3 teaspoons sesame seeds
   Non-stick cooking spray

Squeeze water from tuna and combine with tofu in a bowl. Add egg whites, carrot, green onion, grated ginger, and salt and pepper. Heat a non-stick skillet coated with non-stick cooking spray and add sesame seeds. Shape tuna mixture into 2-inch patties and fry until brown and firm. Makes about 10 2-inch patties.

Nutritional Information

(per serving)

Calories	150
Fat	7 g
Cholesterol	19 mg
Sodium	349 mg

Diabetic Exchanges

Medium-fat meat 2

Tofu Seafood Casserole

1 (6⅛-ounce) can water-packed tuna

4 egg whites

1 large block firm tofu

1 (8-ounce) can water chestnuts, coarsely chopped

4–5 stalks green onion, finely chopped

1 package katsuo dashi no moto (broth mix)

½ teaspoon sesame oil (optional)

1 tablespoon sugar

1½ tablespoons oyster sauce

1½ tablespoons low-sodium shoyu

¼ teaspoon black pepper

3 tablespoons dried shaved bonito

Preheat oven to 350 degrees. Squeeze water from tuna and discard. Mix tuna with egg whites and set aside. Gently squeeze excess water from tofu in a colander, then add to tuna mixture, mashing and mixing together well. Stir in remaining ingredients and blend well. Turn into a casserole dish coated with non-stick cooking spray. Bake for 40 minutes.

Nutritional Information

(per serving)

Calories	185
Fat	6 g
Cholesterol	19 mg
Sodium	690 mg

Diabetic Exchanges

Medium-fat meat	1
Lean meat	2

Tofu and Shrimp

13 ounces firm tofu, drained and cut into 1-inch cubes

1/2 pound shrimp, shelled and deveined

1/3 cup chopped onion

2 cloves garlic, minced

3 tablespoons hoisin sauce

2 tablespoons rice vinegar

2 tablespoons water

2 teaspoons light-brown sugar

1 teaspoon minced ginger

1/2 teaspoon cornstarch

1/8 teaspoon crushed red pepper flakes

2 tablespoons chopped green onion for garnish

Coat a large non-stick skillet with non-stick cooking spray. Heat skillet over medium-high heat and add tofu cubes; stir-fry gently for about 2 minutes. Remove from pan and set aside. Coat skillet again with non-stick cooking spray and stir-fry shrimp, onions and garlic for about 2 minutes. Combine hoisin sauce, vinegar, water, sugar, ginger, red pepper and cornstarch; add to skillet, stirring until thickened. Gently stir in tofu. Sprinkle with chopped green onion and serve.

Nutritional Information

(per serving)

Calories	175
Fat	8 g
Cholesterol	70 mg
Sodium	168 mg

Diabetic Exchanges

Lean meat	1.5
Medium-fat meat	1.0

Stuffed Peppers

4 medium green bell peppers

4 sun-dried tomatoes

6 ounces firm tofu, drained

$1/2$ cup chopped onion

4 cloves garlic, minced

1 teaspoon dried oregano

1 teaspoon dried basil

2 cups cooked rice

$1/4$ cup raisins

$1^1/4$ cup no-salt added tomato sauce

Black pepper to taste

Dash of liquid hot pepper sauce (optional)

Cut tops from peppers and remove seeds and tough inner ribs. Steam 4 minutes to soften slightly, then invert to drain. Place sun-dried tomatoes in boiling water in steamer base and blanch 2 minutes. Drain and chop. Crumble tofu and combine in a skillet with onion and garlic. Sauté over medium-high heat until tofu is dry. Remove from heat and add sun-dried tomatoes, oregano, basil, rice, raisins and 1 cup tomato sauce ; mix well. Fill peppers with tofu-rice mixture and stand upright in a baking pan. Mix $1/4$ cup tomato sauce with pepper and liquid hot pepper sauce; spoon over each pepper. Pour hot water around peppers to a depth of about 1 inch and bake in a 350-degree oven for 40 minutes or until peppers are tender and sauce on top is thick.

Nutritional Information

(per serving)

Calories	255
Fat	4 g
Cholesterol	0 mg
Sodium	112 mg

Diabetic Exchanges

Vegetable	2.0
Bread	1.0
Medium-fat meat	1.0
Fruit	0.5

Stuffed Aburage
with Black Bean Sauce

1 pound lean ground turkey

1 (5-ounce) can water chestnuts, drained and chopped

5 pieces dried shiitake mushrooms, washed, soaked, boiled and chopped

$\frac{1}{2}$ onion, chopped

$\frac{2}{3}$ cup chopped green onion

2 teaspoons oyster sauce

1 teaspoon water

12 pieces aburage triangles

Sauce:

$\frac{1}{4}$ cup low-sodium shoyu

$\frac{1}{4}$ cup water

2 tablespoons salted fermented black beans, rinsed, then mashed with 2 tablespoons water

1 clove garlic

2 teaspoons hoisin sauce

2 teaspoons Szechuan sauce

3 tablespoons cornstarch

$\frac{1}{3}$ cup water

2 teaspoons sugar

Chopped green onion

Combine first seven ingredients. Cut each aburage in half and slit on longest side. Fill with 2 tablespoons turkey mixture. Place in a casserole dish on a steamer rack in a large wok; cover and steam 15 to 20 minutes on medium-high heat. Mix shoyu, $\frac{1}{4}$ cup water, black beans, garlic, hoisin and Szechuan sauces; set aside. Combine cornstarch, $\frac{1}{3}$ cup water and sugar and set aside. Remove aburage from wok. Return four pieces aburage to wok with $\frac{1}{4}$ cup shoyu mixture and $1\frac{1}{2}$ tablespoons cornstarch mixture; saute until most of the sauce is absorbed. Remove to platter and repeat process with remaining aburage; pour any remaining sauce on top. Garnish with green onion.

Nutritional Information

(per serving)

Calories	185
Fat	9 g
Cholesterol	32 mg
Sodium	695 mg

Diabetic Exchanges

Bread	0.5
Lean meat	2.0
Fat	1.0

Tofu with Ground Turkey

1/4 pound lean ground turkey

1/4 cup green onion, cut into 2-inch lengths

1 tablespoon grated ginger

1 1/2 tablespoons hot black bean paste

1 tablespoon dry white wine

2 1/2 tablespoons low-sodium shoyu

2 teaspoons cornstarch

1 tablespoon water

16 ounces firm tofu, cut into 1/2-inch cubes

Chopped green onion

Stir-fry turkey in a non-stick skillet coated with non-stick cooking spray; add green onion. Mix ginger, hot black bean paste, wine, shoyu, cornstarch and water; add to skillet and bring to a simmer. Add tofu and toss gently. Garnish with chopped green onion.

Nutritional Information		Diabetic Exchanges	
(per serving)			
Calories	170	Lean meat	2.5
Fat	9 g	Fat	1.0
Cholesterol	24 mg		
Sodium	630 mg		

Broiled Pork

1 pound lean boneless pork

2 teaspoons chopped ginger

2 tablespoons cooking wine

1¹/₂ tablespoons red hot bean paste

³/₄ teaspoon salt

1 tablespoon sesame oil

2 stalks green onion, minced

2 cloves garlic, minced

¹/₄ teaspoon black pepper

2 tablespoons water

1¹/₂ tablespoons sugar

Slice pork thinly, then marinate in ginger and wine for 10 minutes. Combine red hot bean paste, salt, sesame oil, green onions, garlic, black pepper, water and sugar. Add pork to seasoning mixture and marinate for 15 more minutes. Broil in oven, turning once until cooked through. Serve hot.

Nutritional Information

(per serving)

Calories	140
Fat	5 g
Cholesterol	54 mg
Sodium	307 mg

Diabetic Exchanges

Lean meat	2.5

Pork Chops

6 pork loin chops, 1-inch thick
1/2 cup all-purpose flour
   Olive oil flavored non-stick cooking spray
3 large tomatoes, diced
1 medium onion, chopped
1 cup sliced fresh mushrooms
2 cloves garlic, minced
1/2 cup sherry

1 teaspoon salt
1/4 teaspoon black pepper
1 green bell pepper, sliced crosswise into rings

Dredge pork chops in flour. Coat a large skillet with non-stick cooking spray for about 2 seconds. Heat skillet and fry chops until golden brown on both sides; remove. Add tomatoes to skillet with onion, mushrooms and garlic; sauté for a few minutes, then add sherry, salt and pepper. Return chops to skillet and top with green bell pepper. Cover and simmer about 45 to 50 minutes or until chops are tender.

Nutritional Information		*Diabetic Exchanges*	
(per serving)			
Calories	235	Vegetable	1.0
Fat	9 g	Bread	0.5
Cholesterol	60 mg	Lean meat	3.0
Sodium	503 mg		

Stuffed Eggplant

3 small round eggplants

$^1/_2$ pound very lean ground pork or turkey

2 egg whites

1 tablespoon chopped onion

$^1/_4$ teaspoon minced ginger

2 teaspoons low-sodium shoyu

2 tablespoons sugar, divided

5 tablespoons defatted chicken broth

$^1/_2$ cup miso

Preheat oven to 375 degrees. Coat a baking pan with non-stick cooking spray. Partially peel eggplant (leave lengthwise strips unpeeled), and cut in half lengthwise. (Do not remove stem.) Make a lengthwise slit in each half and rub with salt. Combine turkey, egg whites, onion, ginger, shoyu and 1 teaspoon sugar; pack into slits in eggplant. Place on prepared pan and bake for 30 minutes. Add remaining sugar to broth; stir gradually into miso. Brush sauce over baked eggplant, then broil 3 inches from heat until bubbly. Serve.

Nutritional Information		Diabetic Exchanges	
(per serving)			
Calories	175	Vegetable	1.0
Fat	6 g	Lean meat	2.0
Cholesterol	30 mg	Bread	0.5
Sodium	868 mg		

Pinakbet

¹/₄ pound bittermelon; whole, halved or quartered (depending on size)

¹/₄ pound Japanese eggplant; whole, halved or quartered (depending on size)

¹/₄ pound okra, trimmed

¹/₄ pound string beans, trimmed and cut in 2-inch lengths

¹/₄ cup sliced onion

2 cups cooked lean pork slices

1 cup cherry tomatoes, coarsely chopped

1¹/₂ tablespoons bagoong or fish sauce

¹/₄ cup water

1 2-inch piece ginger, sliced and crushed

Place all ingredients in a large pot; cover and boil a few minutes to wilt vegetables, then toss gently to mix. Reduce heat to low and simmer partially covered, tossing or stirring gently occasionally. Cook to desired doneness.

Nutritional Information

(per serving)

Calories	200
Fat	8 g
Cholesterol	51 mg
Sodium	353 mg

Diabetic Exchanges

Vegetable	2.5
Lean meat	2.5

Pan Pizza

1 pound frozen bread dough, thawed

³/₄ pound Canadian bacon, thinly sliced

1 (12-ounce) can tomato puree

2 teaspoons dried oregano

2 teaspoons dried basil

1 teaspoon thyme

¹/₂ pound fresh mushrooms, thinly sliced

1 medium onion, thinly sliced

1 green bell pepper, thinly sliced

¹/₄ cup grated Parmesan cheese

¹/₄ pound part-skim mozzarella cheese, shredded

Preheat oven to 450 degrees. Spray a 15 x 10-inch jelly roll pan with non-stick cooking spray. Stretch and press dough to fit, making a 1-inch rim on all sides. Cover with a dish towel and set in a warm place for about 20 to 30 minutes or until dough has risen. While dough is rising, combine tomato puree, oregano, basil and thyme in a small saucepan and cook over low heat for about 15 minutes or until slightly thickened. Spread sauce over dough and top with Canadian bacon, mushrooms, onion and green bell pepper. Bake for 10 to 15 minutes. Sprinkle with Parmesan and mozzarella cheeses and bake for another 5 minutes until melted.

Note: To reduce sodium by 650 mg per serving, replace Canadian bacon with vegetable toppings such as zucchini, tomato, spinach, artichoke hearts and green onion. If using a dark-colored pan, you may need to decrease the oven temperature to 400 degrees or decrease baking time.

Nutritional Information		Diabetic Exchanges	
(per serving)			
Calories	240	Vegetable	1.0
Fat	8 g	Bread	1.0
Cholesterol	34 mg	Lean meat	2.0
Sodium	929 mg	Fat	0.5

Beef Stew

1½ pounds lean beef chuck, cut into cubes

¼ cup all-purpose flour

1 tablespoon vegetable oil

1 cup chopped onion

2 cloves garlic, minced

⅔ cup diced celery

¼ cup chopped parsley

½ teaspoon rosemary

½ teaspoon freshly ground black pepper

½ teaspoon thyme

¼ teaspoon oregano

½ cup dry red wine

1 cup water

2 cups chopped tomatoes

4 medium potatoes, quartered

4 cups diced carrots

Dredge beef in flour and brown in oil in a large Dutch oven. Add onion and garlic and cook until onion is soft; pour off fat. Add celery, parsley, rosemary, pepper, thyme, oregano, wine and water. Bring to a boil, cover and simmer for 1 hour. Stir in tomatoes, potatoes and carrots and simmer 45 minutes or until potatoes are tender.

Nutritional Information

(per serving)

Calories	325
Fat	6 g
Cholesterol	66 mg
Sodium	179 mg

Diabetic Exchanges

Vegetable	2.0
Bread	1.5
Lean meat	3.0

Korean Flank Steak

1/3 cup low-sodium shoyu

1/3 cup sugar

1–2 cloves garlic, crushed

1 pound flank steak (have butcher run it through the tenderizer twice)

1/4 cup all-purpose flour

3 egg whites

3 tablespoons chopped green onion

1 tablespoon sesame seeds, toasted

Mix together shoyu, sugar and garlic. Marinate tenderized flank steak in mixture for 20 minutes. Dip in flour, then in egg. Pan fry for about 3 1/2 minutes on each side in a non-stick pan coated with non-stick cooking spray. Cool. Slice into bite-sized strips. Garnish with green onion and sesame seeds.

Nutritional Information

(per serving)

Calories	250
Fat	8 g
Cholesterol	48 mg
Sodium	650 mg

Diabetic Exchanges

Lean meat	3.0
Bread	1.0

Beef with Tomato and Peppers

Serves 6

1 pound top sirloin, thinly sliced
4 tablespoons low-sodium shoyu
2 teaspoons dry sherry or sake
1 teaspoon mirin
2 teaspoons light-brown sugar
1 tablespoon cornstarch
2 cloves garlic, minced
   Salt (optional) and black pepper to taste

1 tablespoon peanut oil
1 medium onion, cut in wedges
2 green bell peppers, sliced
2–3 medium tomatoes, quartered
2 tablespoons chopped green onion

Marinate meat in shoyu, sherry, mirin, sugar, cornstarch, garlic and pepper for 15 minutes. Drain meat (reserve marinade) and stir-fry in oil in a large skillet. Remove meat, then stir-fry onion and green bell pepper for 2 minutes. Return meat to skillet with marinade, tomatoes and green onion. Heat through and serve.

Nutritional Information

(per serving)

Calories	215
Fat	9 g
Cholesterol	58 mg
Sodium	344 mg
	(without salt)

Diabetic Exchanges

Vegetable	1.5
Lean meat	3.0

Spanish Rice

$^1/_2$ pound ground round

1 medium onion, chopped

1 red or green bell pepper, in $^1/_2$-inch dice

2 stalks celery, sliced thinly

2 cloves garlic, minced

1 cup uncooked white rice

1 (14$^1/_2$-ounce) can whole peeled tomatoes, drained and chopped, liquid reserved

$^1/_8$ cup red wine

1 teaspoon dried oregano

1 teaspoon dried thyme

$^1/_2$ teaspoon salt

$^1/_4$ teaspoon ground black pepper

$^1/_8$ teaspoon cayenne pepper

Add enough water to tomato liquid to make 2 cups; set aside. In a large non-stick skillet with a tight-fitting lid, break up ground beef into coarse pieces and brown lightly. Add onion, bell pepper, celery and garlic. Cook, stirring frequently, for about 5 minutes or until vegetables are soft. Stir in rice, chopped tomato, tomato liquid and remaining ingredients. Bring to a boil, then cover and simmer until all liquid is absorbed, about 20 minutes. (Rice should be moist but not soupy.) Remove from heat and let stand, covered, for 5 minutes before serving.

Nutritional Information

(per serving)

Calories	330
Fat	9 g
Cholesterol	27 mg
Sodium	385 mg

Diabetic Exchanges

Vegetable	1.0
Bread	2.5
Lean meat	1.5
Fat	1.0

Grilled Beef and Tofu Kabobs

½ cup dry red wine

3 tablespoons wine vinegar

3 cloves garlic, minced

3 tablespoons minced parsley

½ teaspoon black pepper

1 teaspoon dried oregano

1 teaspoon dried tarragon

¾ pound beef top round steak, in 1½-inch dice

8 ounces firm tofu in 1½-inch dice

1 small red bell pepper in 1-inch dice

1 Maui onion, cut in wedges

1 small zucchini, cut into 1-inch pieces

Combine wine, vinegar, garlic, parsley, pepper, oregano and tarragon; pour over beef and tofu. Marinate 30 minutes. Drain beef and tofu (reserve marinade), and thread on skewers with green bell pepper, onion and zucchini. Grill over hot coals or under the broiler 5 to 8 minutes, or until beef is done and vegetable are tender, turning occasionally and basting with reserved marinade.

Nutritional Information

(per serving)

Calories	230
Fat	9 g
Cholesterol	69 mg
Sodium	66 mg

Diabetic Exchanges

Vegetable	2.0
Lean meat	3.5

Molokai Venison Stew

$^1/_2$ cup all-purpose flour

1 teaspoon salt

Dash of cayenne pepper

2 pounds venison breast or shoulder, cut in
1-inch cubes

1 tablespoon oil

6 cups boiling water

Freshly ground black pepper

4 medium potatoes, diced

4 carrots, diced

2 turnips, diced

4 onions, diced

2 tablespoons all-purpose flour

Combine flour, salt and cayenne pepper in a small bowl. Dredge venison in seasoned flour and brown in a heavy skillet using 1 tablespoon oil. Add boiling water and pepper to browned meat; cover and simmer for 2 to 3 hours. Stir in diced vegetables and cook until tender. Mix 2 tablespoons flour with water to thicken remaining liquid.

Nutritional Information

(per serving)

Calories	300
Fat	4 g
Cholesterol	74 mg
Sodium	378 mg

Diabetic Exchanges

Vegetable	2.0
Bread	1.5
Lean meat	2.5

Meatless Chili

1 large onion, chopped

3 cloves garlic, minced

1 tablespoon canola oil

1¹/₂ cups water

¹/₃ cup pearl barley

1 large green bell pepper, chopped

1 cup chopped fresh mushrooms

2 cups "Light 'n' Tangy" V8 juice

4 small tomatoes, seeded and diced

3 teaspoons chili powder

1 teaspoon paprika

1 teaspoon cumin

1 (15-ounce) can pinto beans, drained and rinsed

1 (15-ounce) can light-red kidney beans, drained and rinsed

2 medium carrots, grated

¹/₂ cup loosely packed Chinese parsley

Juice of 1 lime

Sauté onion and garlic in canola oil on medium heat until onion is almost clear. Add water and barley. Bring to a boil, reduce heat and cover; cook for about 10 minutes. Stir in bell pepper, mushrooms, V8 juice, tomatoes and spices. Cover and cook on medium to medium-high heat for about 15 minutes. Add beans, carrots, Chinese parsley and lime juice. Reduce heat and let stand 30 to 45 minutes to reduce, stirring occasionally. Serve hot over rice and/or topped with diced onion, Chinese parsley or reduced-fat cheese.

Nutritional Information

(per serving)

Calories	365
Fat	4 g
Cholesterol	0 mg
Sodium	586 mg

Diabetic Exchanges

Vegetable	2.5
Bread	3.5
Fat	0.5

Vegetable Laulau

1 pound sweet potatoes, peeled and cut into
   $1/2$-inch cubes

1 pound taro, peeled and cut into $1/2$-inch cubes

8–12 ti leaves

1 pound luau (taro) leaves, separated into
   4 portions

$1/4$ cup low-fat coconut milk or imitation coconut
   milk

Place portions of sweet potatoes and taro on luau leaves; add coconut milk and salt to taste, if desired. Wrap in ti leaves. Steam in pressure cooker for 20 to 25 minutes or until done.

Note: To prevent an allergic reaction when handling raw taro, wear gloves or rub your hands well with cooking oil. No part of the taro plant should be eaten raw because it contains calcium oxalate crystals (calcified nutrients), which break down during cooking.

Nutritional Information		*Diabetic Exchanges*	
(per serving)			
Calories	315	Vegetable	1.0
Fat	1 g	Bread	3.5
Cholesterol	0 mg		
Sodium	120 mg		
(without salt)			

Lentil Stew

1 cup dry lentils

3½ cups defatted, reduced-sodium chicken broth

1 (14½-ounce) can peeled Italian-style tomatoes, cut up (reserve juice)

1 cup peeled and chopped potato

½ cup chopped carrot

½ cup chopped celery

½ cup chopped onion

2 tablespoons chopped parsley

1 tablespoon dried basil, crushed

1 clove garlic, minced

Dash of black pepper

2 tablespoons flour mixed with ¼ cup water

Rinse and drain lentils. Combine lentils with remaining ingredients in a large saucepan and bring to a boil. Reduce heat, cover and simmer for 45 to 50 minutes or until lentils and vegetables are tender, stirring occasionally.

Nutritional Information

(per serving)

Calories	260
Fat	2 g
Cholesterol	0 mg
Sodium	202 mg

Diabetic Exchanges

Bread	2.5
Vegetable	2.0

Spaghetti with Eggplant Sauce

Serves 6

2 tablespoons olive oil
1 onion, sliced
1–3 cloves garlic, minced
1 eggplant, cut into cubes (do not peel)
1 bell pepper, sliced
1 cup chopped tomatoes

1 cup no-salt-added tomato juice
1 teaspoon dried oregano
2 teaspoons dried basil
  Pepper to taste
12 ounces spaghetti

Heat olive oil in a large pot over medium-high heat. Sauté onion and garlic, then add eggplant and bell pepper and sauté 3 minutes or until tender. In a bowl, combine tomatoes, tomato juice and herbs. Add to eggplant mixture. Reduce heat, cover and simmer ½ hour. Cook spaghetti according to package directions, omitting salt. Drain and serve with eggplant sauce.

Nutritional Information		Diabetic Exchanges	
(per serving)			
Calories	280	Vegetable	2
Fat	5 g	Bread	2
Cholesterol	0 mg	Fat	1
Sodium	10 mg		

Spaghetti with Lentil Sauce

$^3/_4$ cup dried lentils

$^1/_2$ cup chopped onion

$^1/_4$ cup sliced mushrooms

$^1/_4$ cup chopped green bell pepper

2 cloves garlic, minced

1 tablespoon olive oil

$^1/_4$ teaspoon liquid hot pepper sauce

$^1/_8$ teaspoon black pepper

2 cups defatted beef broth

$^1/_2$ teaspoon dried basil

$^1/_2$ teaspoon dried oregano

8 ounces canned tomatoes

3 ounces tomato paste

1 tablespoon red wine

12 ounces spaghetti, cooked as directed

Rinse, soak and drain lentils according to package directions. Sauté onion, mushrooms, green bell pepper and garlic in oil in a large saucepan for 5 minutes. Stir in lentils, liquid hot pepper sauce, pepper and broth. Reduce heat, cover and simmer 30 minutes. Add basil, oregano, tomatoes, tomato paste and red wine. Simmer uncovered for about 1 hour, stirring occasionally. Serve over spaghetti.

Nutritional Information		Diabetic Exchanges	
(per serving)			
Calories	345	Vegetable	1
Fat	4 g	Bread	4
Cholesterol	0 mg		
Sodium	528 mg		

Spinach Lasagna

8 ounces lasagna noodles, uncooked

½ cup canned vegetable juice

¼ cup grated Parmesan cheese

Filling:

1 cup non-fat cottage cheese

1 cup low-fat ricotta cheese

1¼ cups shredded part-skim mozzarella cheese

2 egg whites

10 ounces frozen spinach, thawed

Sauce:

2 (30-ounce) jars spaghetti sauce

1 (4-ounce) can mushroom pieces, drained

½ teaspoon dried oregano

⅛ teaspoon black pepper

2 teaspoons dried basil, divided

Combine spaghetti sauce, mushroom pieces, oregano, pepper and 1 teaspoon basil in a large pot. Simmer for 5 minutes on medium heat. In a blender or food processor fitted with a steel blade, process cottage cheese until smooth. Add ricotta, mozzarella, egg whites and remaining 1 teaspoon basil. Squeeze excess water from the spinach and add to cheese mixture; process until thoroughly mixed. In a 13 x 9-inch pan, put a small amount of sauce on the bottom to keep noodles from sticking. Layer one-third of the uncooked noodles, one-third of the sauce and one-third of the filling in the pan. Make two more layers this way, ending with sauce. Pour vegetable juice very carefully around the edges of the lasagna, moving noodles slightly with a spatula to distribute the liquid evenly. Sprinkle with Parmesan cheese. Cover tightly with foil and bake at 350 degrees for 1½ hours.

Note: Use no-salt-added vegetable juice and spaghetti sauce to reduce sodium content.

Nutritional Information		Diabetic Exchanges	
(per serving)			
Calories	300	Vegetable	3.5
Fat	7 g	Bread	1.5
Cholesterol	21 mg	Lean meat	2.0
Sodium	1,160 mg		

Imitation Coconut Cream

2 teaspoons cornstarch

1 cup 2-percent milk

1 teaspoon coconut extract

1/2 package Sweet One (sugar substitute used
   in cooking)

Blend all ingredients together. Use in preparing cooked dishes only.

Nutritional Information		Diabetic Exchanges	
(per 1/2 cup serving)			
Calories	70	Low-fat milk	0.5
Fat	2 g		
Cholesterol	11 mg		
Sodium	61 mg		

Chicken Gravy

2 tablespoons all-purpose flour

$^1/_4$ cup skim milk

1 cup defatted chicken broth

Freshly ground black pepper

Combine flour and skim milk, beating until smooth, or shake mixture in a tightly capped jar. Gradually add to chicken broth in a saucepan. Cook over medium heat, stirring constantly until thick. Add pepper, reduce heat and continue cooking and stirring for 5 minutes.

Nutritional Information   Diabetic Exchanges

(per $^1/_4$ cup serving)

Calories	25	None
Fat	0 g	
Cholesterol	0.5 mg	
Sodium	379 mg	

Barbecue Sauce

1 (8-ounce) can low-sodium tomato sauce
1 tablespoon light-brown sugar
2 tablespoons white vinegar
2 tablespoons minced onion
1½ tablespoons chili powder
1 clove garlic, minced
1 teaspoon dry mustard
1 teaspoon salt (optional)

Combine all ingredients in a small saucepan. Cook over medium heat, stirring constantly, for 15 to 20 minutes or until slightly thickened. Use as a marinade or sauce.

Nutritional Information		Diabetic Exchanges	
(per 2 tablespoon serving)			
Calories	25	Vegetable	0.5
Fat	0 g		
Cholesterol	0 mg		
Sodium	48 mg		
(without salt)			

Tartar Sauce

1 (8-ounce) carton low-fat vanilla yogurt

¼ cup chopped dill pickle or pickle relish

¼ teaspoon black pepper

1 teaspoon minced capers (may substitute dill pickles)

Thoroughly blend all ingredients. Chill at least 1 hour. Use as a dip for seafood, as a vegetable or salad dressing, or in place of mayonnaise on sandwiches.

Nutritional Information

(per 2 tablespoon serving)

Calories	25
Fat	.4 g
Cholesterol	1.5 mg
Sodium	126 mg

Diabetic Exchanges

None

Pickled Papaya

2–3 green papayas, peeled, seeded and grated
(about 5 cups)

$1/2$ cup water

1 tablespoon salt

$1/2$ cup vinegar

$1/2$ cup sugar

$1/2$ teaspoon salt

1 clove garlic, minced

1 tablespoon minced ginger

$1/4$ cup chopped onion

$1/4$ cup julienned carrot

1 small red or green bell pepper, sliced in strips

Mix grated papaya with water and 1 tablespoon salt; let stand for a few hours. Rinse and wrap in cheesecloth a portion at a time; squeeze out excess water. Boil vinegar, sugar and $1/2$ teaspoon salt in a saucepan; add garlic, ginger, onion, carrot and pepper. Boil 5 minutes. Pour hot mixture over papaya and mix well. Refrigerate several hours before serving. Seal in sterilized glass jars for longer storage. Makes 4 cups.

Note: Green papaya may have a yellow tinge.

Nutritional Information

(per 2 tablespoon serving)

Calories	20
Fat	0 g
Cholesterol	0 mg
Sodium	52 mg

Diabetic Exchanges

None

Nā meaʻono

Desserts

Haupia

Original

¹/₂ cup cornstarch
¹/₂ cup sugar
¹/₄ teaspoon salt
 3 cups coconut milk

Reduced

¹/₂ cup cornstarch
¹/₂ cup sugar
¹/₄ teaspoon salt
 1 (13¹/₂-ounce) can coconut milk
1¹/₄ cups whole milk
¹/₂ teaspoon coconut extract

Combine dry ingredients; add coconut milk and whole milk and mix until smooth. Cook over medium heat, stirring constantly until mixture starts to thicken. Lower heat and add coconut extract; cook and stir for 5 minutes. Pour into an 8-inch square pan and refrigerate.

Nutritional Information (per serving)

Original		Reduced	
Calories	120	Calories	100
Fat	9 g	Fat	6 g
Cholesterol	0 mg	Cholesterol	3 mg
Sodium	39 mg	Sodium	46 mg

Diabetic Exchanges

Original		Reduced	
Fruit	1.0	Fruit	1.0
Fat	1.5	Fat	1.0

Banana Bread

Original

- 1 cup vegetable oil
- 2 cups sugar
- 4 eggs
- 3 ripe bananas, mashed
- 1 teaspoon salt
- 2½ cups all-purpose flour
- ½ teaspoon baking powder
- 2 teaspoons baking soda
- ½ cup chopped walnuts

Reduced

- ¾ cup margarine, softened
- 2 cups sugar
- 2 teaspoons each vanilla extract and lemon juice
- 3 eggs, slightly beaten
- 5 ripe bananas, mashed
- ½ teaspoon salt
- 3½ cups all-purpose flour
- 2 teaspoons each baking powder and baking soda
- 1 cup plain non-fat yogurt
- ½ cup chopped walnuts

Preheat oven to 350 degrees. Cream margarine and sugar together in a large bowl. Add vanilla, lemon juice and eggs; beat well. Stir in mashed bananas and set aside. Sift together dry ingredients and combine with banana mixture. Stir in yogurt and nuts. Pour into two loaf pans coated with non-stick cooking spray and bake for 50 minutes or until toothpick inserted into center comes out clean. Cool in pan. Cut each loaf into 16 slices.

Nutritional Information (per serving)

Original		Reduced	
Calories	185	Calories	175
Fat	9 g	Fat	6 g
Cholesterol	26 mg	Cholesterol	20 mg
Sodium	132 mg	Sodium	168 mg

Diabetic Exchanges

Original		Reduced	
Fruit	0.5	Fruit	1.0
Bread	1.0	Bread	1.0
Fat	2.0	Fat	1.0

Layered Manju

Original

 5 cups all-purpose flour

$^1/_2$ cup sugar

$^1/_2$ teaspoon salt

 1 pound (4 sticks) butter

$^3/_4$ cup sweetened condensed milk

 1 (12-ounce) can tsubushi an

 1 (12-ounce) can koshi an

 1 egg

Reduced

 4 cups all-purpose flour

$^1/_3$ cup sugar

$^1/_2$ teaspoon salt

$^3/_4$ pound (3 sticks) margarine

$^2/_3$ cup low-fat sweetened condensed milk

 1 (12-ounce) can tsubushi an

 1 (12-ounce) can koshi an

 1 egg

Preheat oven to 375 degrees. Combine dry ingredients and cream with margarine. Alternately combine dry mixture and milk. Divide dough in half; pat one portion into a 13 x 9-inch pan. Mix tsubushi and koshi an and spread on dough. Spread remaining portion of dough on top and brush with beaten egg. Bake for 35 to 40 minutes.

Nutritional Information (per serving)

Original		Reduced	
Calories	345	Calories	285
Fat	17 g	Fat	12 g
Cholesterol	49 mg	Cholesterol	6 mg
Sodium	195 mg	Sodium	197 mg

Diabetic Exchanges

Original		Reduced	
Fruit	1	Fruit	0.5
Bread	2	Bread	2.0
Fat	3	Fat	2.0

Oreo Cookie Brownies

Original

2 cups Oreo cookie crumbs
(24 cookies without filling)
¼ cup butter, melted
2 cups semi-sweet chocolate chips
1 (14-ounce) can sweetened condensed milk
1 teaspoon vanilla extract
1 cup walnuts, chopped

Reduced

2 cups Oreo cookie crumbs
(24 cookies without filling)
3 tablespoons low-fat margarine
(60% less fat), melted
2 cups semi-sweet chocolate chips
1 (14-ounce) can low-fat sweetened condensed milk
1 teaspoon vanilla extract
¾ cup walnuts, finely chopped

Preheat oven to 350 degrees. Combine cookie crumbs with melted margarine and press firmly into a 13 x 9-inch pan. In a medium saucepan, combine 1 cup chocolate chips, condensed milk and vanilla until chocolate chips are melted. Spread over crust evenly. Sprinkle with remaining chocolate chips and nuts. Bake for 20 minutes. Let cool completely before cutting into bars. Store in an airtight container.

Nutritional Information (per serving)

Original		Reduced	
Calories	210	Calories	155
Fat	11 g	Fat	8 g
Cholesterol	11 mg	Cholesterol	2 mg
Sodium	112 mg	Sodium	97 mg

Diabetic Exchanges

Original		Reduced	
Fruit	0.5	Fruit	0.5
Bread	1.0	Bread	1.0
Fat	2.0	Fat	1.0

Oatmeal Cookies

¹/₂ cup firmly packed light-brown sugar

¹/₃ cup margarine, softened

¹/₂ cup liquid egg substitute

1 teaspoon vanilla extract

1 cup quick cooking oats

1 cup crisp rice cereal

³/₄ cup all-purpose flour

1 teaspoon cinnamon

¹/₂ teaspoon baking soda

¹/₄ cup raisins

¹/₄ cup diced dried apricots

Preheat oven to 350 degrees. Beat brown sugar and margarine with an electric mixer until creamy. On medium speed, beat in egg substitute and vanilla. In another bowl, mix oats, rice cereal, flour, cinnamon and baking soda; stir into sugar mixture. Add raisins and apricots and mix well. Drop dough by rounded tablespoonfuls onto baking sheet coated with non-stick cooking spray. Bake for 8 to 10 minutes or until lightly browned. Cool completely on wire racks.

Makes 24 cookies

Nutritional Information		Diabetic Exchanges	
(per cookie)			
Calories	75	Bread	1
Fat	2 g		
Cholesterol	0 mg		
Sodium	59 mg		

Biscotti

Non-stick cooking spray
2 cups all-purpose flour
2 teaspoons baking powder
2 teaspoons anise seed, crushed

1 teaspoon grated lemon peel
$^1/_4$ cup margarine
$^1/_2$ cup sugar
2 eggs

Preheat oven to 375 degrees. Coat a large baking sheet with non-stick cooking spray; set aside. Stir together flour, baking powder, anise seed and lemon peel; set aside. In a mixing bowl, beat margarine with an electric mixer on medium speed until softened. Add sugar; beat until fluffy. Add eggs and beat well. Stir in flour mixture. On waxed paper, shape dough into two 12-inch logs. Place on prepared baking sheet and slightly flatten logs. Bake 15 to 20 minutes or until lightly browned. Cool completely on wire racks (about 1 hour). Cut each log into $^1/_2$-inch slices. Arrange slices, cut side down, on baking sheet. Bake at 300 degrees for 10 minutes. Turn over, bake 5 to 10 minutes longer or until crisp and dry. Cool completely on wire racks.
Makes 48 cookies.

Nutritional Information		Diabetic Exchanges	
(per 2 cookie serving)			
Calories	80	Bread	1
Fat	2 g		
Cholesterol	22 mg		
Sodium	54 mg		

Black Forest Fudge Cake

2 cups cake flour

1 cup unsweetened cocoa

1 teaspoon baking powder

½ teaspoon salt

1½ cups firmly packed dark-brown sugar

2 eggs

1 egg white

1 cup prune puree*

¾ cup skim milk

1 cup boiling water

2 tablespoon espresso coffee poweder

2 teaspoons baking soda

2 cups frozen, pitted, unsweetened dark sweet cherries, coarsely chopped, thawed and well-drained

¼ cup chopped toasted walnuts

Garnish: powdered sugar, additional cherries (fresh or frozen), mint sprig

Preheat oven to 350 degrees. Coat a 3- to 4-quart bundt pan with non-stick cooking spray. Sift together flour, cocoa, baking powder and salt; stir in brown sugar and set aside. In another bowl, whisk eggs with prune puree, milk and vanilla; set aside. Pour boiling water into a measuring cup; stir in espresso powder and baking soda. Stir egg mixture into flour mixture; mix just until blended. Pour half the batter into prepared pan; sprinkle evenly with cherries and walnuts. Carefully pour in remaining batter. Bake about 45 minutes. Invert onto a rack and cool completely. Dust with powdered sugar. Fill cake center with additional cherries and garnish with mint.

*To make prune puree, place pitted prunes in a blender with just enough water to make an applesauce-like consistency.

Nutritional Information		Diabetic Exchanges	
(per serving)			
Calories	210	Fruit	2.0
Fat	3 g	Bread	1.0
Cholesterol	27 mg	Fat	0.5
Sodium	218 mg		

Chocolate Cake

1 cup firmly packed light-brown sugar

$^3/_4$ cup sugar

1 cup all-purpose flour

$^3/_4$ cup liquid egg substitute

$^1/_2$ cup margarine, melted

$^1/_4$ cup unsweetened cocoa

$1^1/_2$ teaspoons vanilla extract

$^1/_3$ cup chopped walnuts

Preheat oven to 350 degrees. In large bowl, combine sugars, flour, egg substitute, margarine and cocoa; mix well. Stir in vanilla and walnuts. Spread mixture into a 13 x 9-inch pan coated with non-stick cooking spray. Bake for 25 minutes or until done. Cool in pan on wire rack. Wrap and store refrigerated for up to 1 week.

Nutritional Information		Diabetic Exchanges	
(per serving)			
Calories	80	Fruit	1.0
Fat	3 g	Fat	0.5
Cholesterol	0 mg		
Sodium	38 mg		

Chocolate Angel Cake

1$^1/_2$ cups egg whites (10–12 large eggs)
  1 cup sifted cake flour or sifted all-purpose flour
1$^1/_2$ cups sifted powdered sugar
  3 tablespoons unsweetened cocoa
 $^1/_2$ teaspoon cinnamon
1$^1/_2$ teaspoons cream of tartar
  1 teaspoon vanilla extract
  1 cup sugar

Preheat oven to 350 degrees. Bring egg whites to room temperature (about 1 hour). Meanwhile, sift flour, powdered sugar, cocoa and cinnamon together three times; set aside. In a large bowl, beat egg whites, cream of tartar and vanilla with an electric mixer on medium speed until soft peaks form (tips curl). Gradually add sugar, 2 tablespoons at a time, beating on high speed until stiff peaks form (tips stand straight). Transfer to a larger bowl, if necessary. Sift about one-fourth of the flour mixture over the beaten egg whites; fold in gently. Repeat, folding in remaining flour mixture by fourths. Pour into an ungreased 10-inch tube pan. Bake on lowest rack in oven for 40 to 45 minutes or when top springs back when lightly touched. Immediately invert cake (leave in pan) and cool completely. To remove cake, loosen sides from pan with a knife.

Nutritional Information		Diabetic Exchanges	
(per serving)			
Calories	120	Bread	1
Fat	0 g	Fruit	1
Cholesterol	0 mg		
Sodium	39 mg		

Gingerbread

3 tablespoons applesauce or prune puree*

1/2 cup dark-brown sugar

1/2 cup dark molasses

1 large egg and two egg whites, lightly beaten

1/2 cup strong brewed coffee

2 teaspoons vanilla extract

1 1/2 teaspoons grated lemon peel

4 teaspoons grated ginger

1 cup grated carrots

1/2 cup raisins, soaked in boiling water
for 10 minutes and drained

1/2 cup whole wheat flour

1 1/2 cups all-purpose flour

2 teaspoons cinnamon

1 1/2 teaspoons baking soda

1 teaspoon ground cloves

1 teaspoon ground allspice

Preheat oven to 350 degrees. Coat a 9-inch square baking pan with non-stick cooking spray. Using an electric mixture or food processor, mix the first 10 ingredients. In a separate bowl, combine remaining dry ingredients and add to wet mixture. Stir just until combined. Pour into baking pan and bake for 45 minutes or until tester inserted into the center comes out clean. Serve with light whipped topping, if desired.

* To make prune puree, place pitted prunes in a blender with just enough water to make an applesauce-like consistency.

Nutritional Information		Diabetic Exchanges	
(per serving)			
Calories	230	Bread	1
Fat	1 g	Fruit	2
Cholesterol	24 mg	Vegetable	1
Sodium	183 mg		

Bread Pudding

Serves
18

3 green apples, pared, cored, chopped in ½-inch pieces

14 cups fresh whole wheat bread crumbs

16 ounces liquid egg substitute

4 cups skim milk

1 cup sugar

½ cup dark-brown sugar

1½ tablespoons cinnamon

1 teaspoon nutmeg

1 cup raisins

2 teaspoons vanilla extract

Preheat oven to 375 degrees. Bring one quart water to a boil in a saucepan. Add chopped apples and cook for 2 minutes. Drain and rinse with cold water; set aside. Combine remaining ingredients; stir in apples. Turn into a non-stick 13 x 9-inch pan and refrigerate overnight. Bake for 1 hour. Cool and cut into serving pieces.

Nutritional Information
(per serving)

Calories	220
Fat	2 g
Cholesterol	1 mg
Sodium	290 mg

Diabetic Exchanges

Fruit	1.5
Bread	1.5
Medium-fat meat	0.5

Sweet Rice

5 cups (use rice cooker measure) mochi rice
5 cups (use rice cooker measure) water
1 (12 ounce) can frozen coconut milk, thawed
1 (1 pound) box light-brown sugar

Wash mochi rice and cook with water in a rice cooker. In large skillet, boil coconut milk until white curdles and oil appears. Stir in brown sugar and boil for 5 minutes. Add cooked mochi rice and mix thoroughly. Cook on low heat for another 5 minutes, stirring occasionally. Spread evenly in a 13 x 9-inch pan. Cool and cut into 32 pieces.

Nutritional Information		Diabetic Exchanges	
(per serving)			
Calories	160	Fruit	1.0
Fat	3 g	Bread	1.0
Cholesterol	0 mg	Fat	0.5
Sodium	10 mg		

Microwave Mochi

1¹/₂ cups mochiko (rice flour)

1¹/₂ cups water

 ¹/₂ cup sugar

   Katakuriko (potato starch) or cornstarch

 6 ounces tsubushi an (or tsubushi an and fresh
   strawberry, or tsubushi an and peanut butter)

Mix mochiko, water and sugar. Lightly coat a small microwaveable tube pan (or round dish with a cup placed in the center) with non-stick cooking spray. Pour mochiko mixture into pan. Microwave for 3 minutes on low, 3 minutes on medium and finally 3 minutes on high. While hot, turn onto a plate sprinkled with katakuriko. Divide into 12 pieces. Dust hands with katakuriko and flatten each piece. Place 1 tablespoon tsubushi an in center; bring edges together and pinch to seal. Shape into a flattened round.

Nutritional Information		Diabetic Exchanges	
(per mochi)			
Calories	110	Fruit	0.5
Fat	0 g	Bread	1.0
Cholesterol	0 mg		
Sodium	3 mg		

Pumpkin Loaf

¾ cup firmly packed light-brown sugar

¼ cup margarine

½ cup liquid egg substitute

1 cup canned pumpkin

⅓ cup skim milk

1 teaspoon vanilla extract

2 cups all-purpose flour

2 teaspoons baking powder

1½ teaspoons pumpkin pie spice

¼ teaspoon baking soda

1 cup raisins

Preheat oven to 350 degrees. In a large bowl, beat brown sugar and margarine at high speed until creamy. At medium speed, beat in egg substitute, pumpkin, milk and vanilla. In small bowl, mix flour, baking powder, pumpkin pie spice and baking soda; stir into pumpkin mixture just until moistened. Stir in raisins. Spoon batter into 8 x 4 x 2½-inch loaf pan coated with non-stick cooking spray. Bake for 65 to 70 minutes or until toothpick inserted in center comes out clean. Cool in pan 10 minutes, remove from pan and cool completely on wire rack.

Nutritional Information		Diabetic Exchanges	
(per serving)			
Calories	155	Bread	1
Fat	2 g	Fruit	1
Cholesterol	0 mg		
Sodium	108 mg		

Sweet Potato Orange Muffins

1 cup all-purpose flour

1 cup whole wheat flour

2 teaspoons baking powder

2 teaspoons baking soda

1 teaspoon cinnamon

1/2 teaspoon nutmeg

1/2 teaspoon allspice

1 (16-ounce) can sweet potatoes (yams), drained

2/3 cup firmly packed dark-brown sugar

2 eggs

1 cup orange juice

1 carrot, shredded

1 teaspoon vanilla extract

Preheat oven to 400 degrees. Coat muffin tin with non-stick cooking spray. Combine flours, baking powder, baking soda, cinnamon, nutmeg and allspice. In another bowl, mash sweet potatoes and stir in sugar, eggs, orange juice, carrots and vanilla. Add dry ingredients to wet ingredients and mix just until blended. Fill muffin tins 3/4 full. Bake 15 to 20 minutes or until tops are brown. Let cool and remove from tins.
Makes 16 to 18 muffins.

Nutritional Information		Diabetic Exchanges	
(per muffin)			
Calories	140	Fruit	1
Fat	1 g	Bread	1
Cholesterol	27 mg		
Sodium	179 mg		

Oat Bran Apple Muffins

1¼ cups whole wheat flour

1 cup oat bran

½ cup firmly packed dark-brown sugar

2½ teaspoons baking powder

¼ teaspoon baking soda

¼ teaspoon salt

¼ teaspoon nutmeg

½ teaspoon cinnamon

1 cup buttermilk

2 egg whites

2 tablespoons vegetable oil

¾ cup peeled, shredded apple

Non-stick cooking spray

Preheat oven to 375 degrees. Stir together flour, oat bran, brown sugar, baking powder, baking soda, salt, nutmeg and cinnamon. In another bowl, combine buttermilk, egg whites and oil; add to dry ingredients and stir just until moistened. Stir in shredded apple. (If desired, store batter, tightly covered, in refrigerator for up to five days.) To bake, coat muffin tin lightly with non-stick cooking spray; fill ¾ full with batter. Bake for 18 to 20 minutes or until a toothpick inserted in center comes out clean.
Makes 12 muffins.

Nutritional Information

(per muffin)

Calories	115
Fat	3 g
Cholesterol	1 mg
Sodium	170 mg

Diabetic Exchanges

Fruit	0.5
Bread	1.0
Fat	0.5

Lemon Crepes

¹/₂ cup all-purpose flour
¹/₄ teaspoon salt
 1 egg
¹/₂ cup whole milk
¹/₂ cup water
 2 tablespoons sugar
 1 lemon

Mix flour and salt in a medium bowl. Beat egg with milk; gradually add to dry ingredients, mixing until smooth.
Add water and blend well. Heat an 8-inch omelette pan coated with non-stick cooking spray over high heat. Pour
2 tablespoons batter into pan, tilting pan until bottom is evenly coated. Cook until edges start to brown; turn and
lightly brown other side. Place on flat surface and sprinkle with ³/₄ teaspoon sugar and lemon juice to taste.
Roll crepe, starting from one end. Serve immediately.

Nutritional Information		Diabetic Exchanges	
(per 2 crepe serving)			
Calories	120	Bread	1.0
Fat	2 g	Fat	0.5
Cholesterol	56 mg		
Sodium	166 mg		

Lemon Bars

³/₄ cup all-purpose flour

¹/₈ cup powdered sugar

¹/₈ cup granulated sugar

¹/₂ cup low-fat margarine

³/₄ cup granulated sugar

 2 tablespoons all-purpose flour

¹/₂ teaspoon baking powder

1 egg

2 egg whites

4–6 tablespoons lemon juice

Preheat oven to 350 degrees. Combine ³/₄ cup flour, ¹/₈ cup powdered sugar and ¹/₈ cup granulated sugar in a bowl. Cut margarine into flour mixture with a pastry blender and pat into bottom of an 8-inch square pan. Bake for 15 minutes. Stir together ³/₄ cup granulated sugar, 2 tablespoons flour and baking powder. Add egg, egg whites and lemon juice; blend well. Pour onto hot baked crust and return to oven for 25 minutes. Cool and cut into bars. Sprinkle with powdered sugar.

Nutritional Information		Diabetic Exchanges	
(per serving)			
Calories	80	Fruit	1.0
Fat	3 g	Fat	0.5
Cholesterol	9 mg		
Sodium	61 mg		

Pineapple Cheesecake

1 cup graham cracker crumbs

2 tablespoons reduced-fat margarine, melted

1 tablespoon oil

1 (3-ounce) package pineapple or lemon gelatin

1 cup boiling water

3 cups non-fat cottage cheese (1^1/$_2$ pounds)

^{1}/$_4$ cup sugar

1 (8^1/$_2$-ounce) can crushed pineapple in juice, undrained

1 tablespoon water

2 teaspoons cornstarch

Combine graham cracker crumbs, margarine and oil; press into bottom of an 8-inch springform pan. Chill. Dissolve gelatin in boiling water and cool to lukewarm. In a food processor or blender, thoroughly mix cottage cheese and sugar. Slowly add gelatin and blend well. Pour mixture into chilled crust and refrigerate until firm. In a saucepan, bring crushed pineapple and juice, water and cornstarch to a boil, stirring constantly. Cool 15 minutes and spread over top of cheesecake. Chill at least 1 hour.

Nutritional Information		Diabetic Exchanges	
(per serving)			
Calories	135	Fruit	1.5
Fat	3 g	Lean meat	1.0
Cholesterol	2 mg		
Sodium	272 mg		

Tropical Cheesecake

3 cups non-fat yogurt

10 graham crackers, crushed to fine crumbs

2 ripe bananas, mashed

4 tablespoons dehydrated coconut milk powder

2 tablespoons powdered sugar

1 teaspoon vanilla or rum extract (optional)

1 stick kanten (agar agar), broken into pieces

1 (20-ounce) can crushed pineapple, drained (juice reserved)

Yogurt cheese: Place yogurt in a strainer lined with a coffee filter or cheesecloth. Cover, set over a bowl and place in refrigerator overnight to let liquid drain.

Bottom layer: Mix graham cracker crumbs with banana and pat evenly on bottom of an 8-inch pan. Freeze.

Cheese filling: Beat 2 cups yogurt cheese with an electric mixer on low speed. Add coconut milk powder, powdered sugar and vanilla or rum extract; beat for one minute. Spread evenly on frozen bottom layer. Cover tightly with foil and return to freezer for at least 2 hours. (The cheesecake can be frozen at this point for up to two weeks.)

Top layer: Combine kanten with pineapple juice in a one-quart saucepan; let soak 30 minutes. Heat over medium heat until mixture begins to bubble. Turn heat to low, stir and simmer 5 minutes or until kanten dissolves completely. Add pineapple and remove from heat. Cool to lukewarm or until just beginning to thicken. Remove cheesecake from freezer and pour pineapple mixture over cheese filling. Cover and refrigerate until ready to serve. (Top layer should be firm in 15 minutes.)

Nutritional Information		Diabetic Exchanges	
(per serving)			
Calories	145	Fruit	1.5
Fat	2 g	Lean meat	1.0
Cholesterol	2 mg		
Sodium	109 mg		

Lilikoi Cream Tarts

1 box phyllo dough
   Non-stick cooking spray
$^2/_3$ cup lilikoi juice concentrate
$^1/_4$ cup sugar
$^1/_4$ cup cornstarch

1 cup plain non-fat yogurt
Garnish: mint leaves, fresh mango, papaya,
   strawberries or mandarin orange

Thaw phyllo dough according to package directions. To make cups, layer four 5-inch square phyllo leaves sprayed with non-stick cooking spray and sprinkled with a little sugar. Press into muffin tin and bake as directed on package. Add enough water to lilikoi juice concentrate to make $1^1/_2$ cups. Pour into a small saucepan and heat with sugar. Mix cornstarch with $^1/_2$ cup water and stir into warm juice. Bring to a boil, stirring constantly, then remove from heat and cool. Whip in yogurt and chill. Spoon into phyllo cups and garnish with mint and fresh fruit just before serving.

Nutritional Information		Diabetic Exchanges	
(per serving)			
Calories	145	Fruit	1
Fat	1 g	Bread	1
Cholesterol	1 mg		
Sodium	141 mg		

Ice Cream Gelatin Surprise

2 (6-ounce) packages strawberry gelatin
1 packet unflavored gelatin
2 tablespoons sugar
1 quart boiling water
1 quart vanilla ice cream, softened

In a large bowl, combine strawberry and unflavored gelatin, sugar and boiling water, stirring until dissolved. Into a small bowl, stir 1 cup of the hot gelatin into ice cream. Gently fold mixture into remaining gelatin. Pour into a 13 x 9-inch pan and chill until firm. Gelatin will form two layers.

Nutritional Information		*Diabetic Exchanges*	
(per serving)			
Calories	135	Bread	1
Fat	3 g	Fat	1
Cholesterol	12 mg		
Sodium	52 mg		

Mango Ice

2 cups mango
$^1/_3$ cup sugar
$^1/_3$ cup lime juice
$^1/_3$ cup triple sec or orange juice
    Lime juice or mint leaves as garnish

Mix all ingredients together. Pour into a shallow dish and freeze. Place frozen mixture in food processor and blend to desired consistency (or fluff with a fork). Garnish and serve immediately.

Nutritional Information

(per serving)

Calories	130
Fat	0 g
Cholesterol	0 mg
Sodium	2 mg

Diabetic Exchanges

Fruit	2

Papaya Sherbet

Serves 2	Serves 24	
1	12	medium papayas, cut into 1-inch pieces and frozen
3 tablespoons	2¼	cups plain low-fat yogurt
1 tablespoon	¾	cup grated lemon rind
3 teaspoons	½	cup frozen apple juice concentrate

Place frozen pieces of papaya in blender. Add yogurt, lemon rind and apple juice concentrate; blend until smooth.

Nutritional Information
(per ½ cup serving)

Calories	120
Fat	1 g
Cholesterol	1 mg
Sodium	26 mg

Diabetic Exchanges

Bread	1
Fruit	2

Almond Float

1½ envelopes unflavored gelatin

⅓ cup cold water

1 cup boiling water

½ cup sugar

½ cup evaporated skim milk

¾ teaspoon almond extract

1 (15-ounce) can fruit cocktail in light syrup or fruit juice

½ cup fresh orange or melon

Optional: Fresh or canned lychees (drained), pitted

In a bowl, soften gelatin in cold water. Add boiling water and sugar and stir until dissolved. Pour in evaporated skim milk and almond extract and mix well. Pour mixture into an 8-inch square baking pan; chill until set. Cut into squares and mix gently with canned fruits, fruit syrup and fresh fruits.

Nutritional Information

(per serving)

Calories	215
Fat	0 g
Cholesterol	1 mg
Sodium	46 mg

Diabetic Exchanges

Fruit	1.5
Skim milk	0.5

Appendices

What is Good Nutrition?

What we eat plays a big part in our health. When we're healthy, we feel good about ourselves and have more energy. Here are some guidelines to follow each day.

- Eat a variety of good food.
  No single food can meet all your health needs.

- Maintain a healthy weight.
  Overeating and too little exercise leads to weight gain, but weighing too little can also lead to health problems.

- Eat less fat and cholesterol.
  A diet high in fat and cholesterol can lead to heart disease and some forms of cancer.

- Eat more fruits, vegetables and complex carbohydrates.
  These foods provide vitamins, minerals and fiber.

- Eat less sweets.
  Foods high in sugar provide calories with little nutritional value.

- Use less salt.
  For some people, eating too much salt will lead to high blood pressure.

- Don't drink too much alcohol.
  Alcohol provides little nutritional value.

Reduced-fat Cooking Methods

Learning a few basic tricks can help you prepare leaner versions of your favorite recipes. Here are some tips:

Braise. Many recipes for soups, stews and sauces begin with chopped vegetables sauteed in butter or oil to develop a flavor base. To get this satisfying flavor with little or no fat, do one of the following instead:

1. Use $1/4$ or $1/2$ the specified amount.
2. Use non-stick cooking spray to coat a non-stick pan.
3. Omit the fat altogether. Instead, add enough liquid to barely cover the vegetables. Boil uncovered over high or medium-high heat, stirring occasionally until the liquid cooks away and the vegetables begin to brown and stick to the pan. Then add more liquid, 2 tablespoons at a time, stirring to release the browned bits from the pan. Repeat this process until the color is rich and appealing; watch closely to prevent scorching.

Oven-fry. Brown small pieces of food (such as meatballs, cut-up chicken or meat, or sliced vegetables) arranged in a single layer on a baking pan lightly coated with non-stick cooking spray. Place in a hot oven (400 to 500 degrees), or under a broiler; watch carefully for doneness. Be sure to leave enough space between the pieces to let moisture evaporate quickly.

Fill in with water. Make smooth sauces by replacing some or all of the butter, margarine or oil with slightly thickened water or other liquid. For each cup of liquid, use:

1 tablespoon flour for a thin sauce
2 tablespoons flour for a medium sauce
3 to 4 tablespoons flour for a thick sauce

If using cornstarch, arrowroot or potato starch, use half the amounts listed above.

Use defatted broths and soups. Chill homemade and canned broth and soup, then skim off the fat that forms on the top. Store cans of broth in the refrigerator so they will always be ready to defat when needed.

Replace the oil called for in muffins, cookies or bars with applesauce or mashed ripe banana.

Be adventurous. Experiment with herbs, spices, fruit or vegetables and their juices for extra flavor.

Lower-fat Choices

Instead of	Choose
Bacon	Canadian bacon
Beef, regular ground	Extra-lean ground beef or lean ground poultry (or half of each)
Cheese	Part-skim mozzarella, part-skim ricotta, reduced-fat cottage cheese, or Parmesan in small amounts
Chicken, whole	Skinned chicken breast
Chocolate, unsweetened	For each ounce, use 3 tablespoons unsweetened cocoa
Whole milk	Skim milk
Cream	Evaporated skim milk
Whole egg	2 egg whites
Ice cream	Frozen reduced-fat yogurt or fruit ices
Mayonnaise	Reduced-calorie mayonnaise or half plain non-fat yogurt and half mayonnaise
Salad dressings	Reduced-fat varieties or homemade with little or no oil
Sour cream	Non-fat sour cream or non-fat yogurt
Tuna or sardines in oil	Tuna or sardines in water

Diabetic Exchanges for Meal Planning

The diabetic exchanges were developed by the American Diabetes Association, Inc. (ADA, Inc.) and the American Dietetic Association (ADA). This meal planning system allows variety in meal plans while maintaining consistent calorie and nutrient levels.

There are six exchange lists or food groups: starch/bread, meat, vegetables, fruit, milk and fats. The foods in each list have similar amount of calories, carbohydrate, protein and fat, based on the listed portion size. A food on the list may be substituted or "exchanged" for another food on the same list. Meal plans can be personalized to meet an individual's health needs and food preferences.

To learn how to use the diabetic exchanges or to develop a personalized meal plan, contact your local American Diabetes Association office or a registered dietitian.

Ma Ke 'Ano Kuloko
Healthy Cooking — Island Style

Name _____ Daytime Phone_____

Address _____

City _____ State _____ Zip _____

	Local	Out-of-State
Price per book:	$10.00	$10.00
Shipping and handling:	2.00	4.00
Total cost per book:	$12.00	$14.00

Number of copies _____   Amount enclosed $ _____

Make checks payable to: Hawaii Nutrition Council. Please do not send cash. Sorry, no c.o.d.s. Project LEAN Hawaii, c/o Hawaii Nutrition Council, P.O. Box 61622, Honolulu, HI 96839-1622.

Profits from the sale of these cookbooks are used to support the purpose and programs of Project LEAN Hawaii, a Hawaii Nutrition Council committee.

Ma Ke 'Ano Kuloko
Healthy Cooking—Island Style

Project LEAN Hawaii would appreciate your feedback on Ma Ke 'Ano Kuloko by completing this questionnaire.

1. Why did you purchase this cookbook? (Check as many as apply.)
    ❏ New recipe ideas   ❏ Local recipes   ❏ Chronic health problems
    ❏ Weight management   ❏ Low-sodium, low-fat or low-cholesterol recipes
    ❏ Gift   ❏ Other (Please specify) _____

2. How did you find out about this cookbook? (Check as many as apply.)
    ❏ Family or friend   ❏ Special event or class   ❏ Media
    ❏ Gift   ❏ Other (Please specify) _____

3. Has the cookbook helped you reduce the fat, cholesterol or sodium in your diet? ❏ Yes   ❏ No

4. Have you been able to modify the fat content of your own recipes using the guidelines in the cookbook?   ❏ Yes ❏ No

5. Would you purchase future editions of reduced-fat local recipes? ❏ Yes   ❏ No

6. Additional comments:_____

Please mail to: **Project LEAN Hawaii**, c/o Hawaii Nutrition Council, P.O. Box 61622, Honolulu, HI 96839-1622. MAHALO!

Index

Korean Flank Steak, 129
Laulau, 83
Lentil Stew, 136
Linguine with Clam Sauce, 100
Mango Chutney Chicken, 108
Meatless Chili, 134
Molokai Venison Stew, 133
Nori Salmon, 95
Ono Zesty Chicken, 109
Oriental Chicken and Vegetables, 102
Pan Pizza, 127
Pancit, 112
Pinakbet, 126
Plum Chicken, 107
Pork Chops, 124
Red Clam Sauce
  with Angel Hair Pasta, 101
Salmon Hot Pot, 96
Shrimp with Black Beans, 98
Shrimp Curry, 86
Simmered Onaga with Somen, 90
Spaghetti with Eggplant Sauce, 137
Spaghetti with Lentil Sauce, 138
Spanish Rice, 131
Spinach Lasagna, 139
String Beans, Carrots and Shrimp, 97

Stuffed Aburage
  with Black Bean Sauce, 121
Stuffed Eggplant, 125
Stuffed Peppers, 120
Sweet Barbecue Chicken, 106
Tofu with Ground Turkey, 122
Tofu Seafood Casserole, 118
Tofu with Tomatoes, 116
Tofu and Shrimp, 119
Tofu and Vegetable Stir-fry, 115
Tuna Tofu Patties, 117
Turkey Adobo, 114
Vegetable Chicken Stir-fry, 103
Vegetable Laulau, 135

Mango

Mango Ice, 169
Mango Chutney Chicken, 108

Muffins

Oat Bran Apple Muffins, 162
Sweet Potato Orange Muffins, 161

Mushrooms

Stuffed Mushrooms, 3
Fresh Mushroom Soup, 50

Noodles/Pasta

Chicken Long Rice, 110
Chow Fun, 61
Chow Mein, 64
Easy Crab Salad, 22
Linguine with Clam Sauce, 100
Pancit, 112
Pasta Salad, 25
Pasta and Bean Soup, 44
Red Clam Sauce
  with Angel Hair Pasta, 101
Simmered Onaga with Somen, 90
Spaghetti with Eggplant Sauce, 137
Spaghetti with Lentil Sauce, 138
Spicy Peanut Noodles, 77
Spinach and Noodle Soup, 49
Spinach Lasagna, 139
Won Bok Chicken Salad, 31

Papaya

Green Papaya Salad, 32
Papaya Seed Salad Dressing, 38
Papaya Sherbet, 170
Pickled Papaya, 144

Side Dishes

Bara Sushi, 76
Barbecue Baked Beans, 78
Bean Sprout Sanbaizu, 73
Broccoli with Oyster Sauce, 72
Char Siu Bao, 80
Chinese Taro Cake, 62
Chow Fun, 61
Chow Mein, 64
Cornbread, 66
Cucumber Namasu, 67
Japanese Pumpkin, 68
Miso Bittermelon, 70
Oriental Vegetable Dish, 69
Oven Baked French Fries, 79
Snow Peas Oriental, 75
Spicy Eggplant, 71
Spicy Peanut Noodles, 77
Watercress and Bean Sprouts
    with Sesame Sauce, 74

Soups

Beef Barley Soup, 57
Black Bean Soup, 45
Chinese Cabbage Soup, 48
Corn and Pepper Soup, 52
Creamy Carrot Soup, 47
Egg Drop Soup, 51
Fish Sabaw, 55
Fishcake Miso Soup, 53
Fresh Mushroom Soup, 50
Minestrone, 46
Mundoo Soup, 56
Oriental Split Pea Soup, 43
Pasta and Bean Soup, 44
Portuguese Bean Soup, 41
Shrimp and Fish Soup, 54
Spinach and Noodle Soup, 49

Spinach

Spinach and Noodle Soup, 49
Spinach Lasagna, 139
Spinach Rolls, 4
Spinach Salad, 35

Tofu

Chinese Cabbage Soup, 48
Fishcake Miso Soup, 53
Grilled Beef and Tofu Kabobs, 132
Mundoo Soup, 56
Stuffed Aburage
    with Black Bean Sauce, 121
Stuffed Peppers, 120
Tofu with Ground Turkey, 122
Tofu Poke, 10
Tofu Seafood Casserole, 118
Tofu and Shrimp, 119
Tofu with Tomatoes, 116
Tofu-Tuna-Tomato Salad, 29
Tofu and Vegetable Stir fry, 115
Tuna Tofu Patties, 117

Vegetarian

Lentil Stew, 136
Meatless Chili, 134
Spaghetti with Eggplant Sauce, 137
Spaghetti with Lentil Sauce, 138
Spinach Lasagna, 139
Vegetable Laulau, 135